Twayne's English Authors Series

Sylvia E. Bowman, *Editor*

INDIANA UNIVERSITY

George William Russell ("AE")

TEAS 208

George William Russell ("AE")

GEORGE WILLIAM RUSSELL ("AE")

By ROBERT BERNARD DAVIS *1917-*

Tarkio College
Tarkio, Missouri

TWAYNE PUBLISHERS
A Division of G. K. Hall & Co.
Boston, Massachusetts, U. S. A.

Library of Congress Cataloging in Publication Data

Davis, Robert Bernard, 1917 -
　George William Russell ("AE")

　(Twayne's English authors series ; TEAS 208)
　Bibliography:　p. 155 - 58
　Includes index.
　1.　Russell, George William, 1867 - 1935—Criticism and inter-
pretation.
PR6035.U7Z576　　　828'.8'09　　　77-4873
ISBN 0-8057-6677-4

To
Alan, Margot, and Charlie
Good Friends
in the Summer of 1964
When It All Began

Contents

About the Author

This book originated in 1964, when Professor Robert Bernard Davis visited England and Ireland and met Alan Denson, the author of the *Bibliography* and the *Letters* of AE. In Ireland, Professor Davis visited the places that AE knew, talked with persons who knew him, and collected the material for the book, chiefly at the National Library of Ireland and the Armagh County Museum. Mr. Denson was helpful in advising Professor Davis and in reading the manuscript.

Professor Davis teaches at Tarkio College in Missouri, where he is Professor of Literature. He was Chairman of the Division of Language and Literature from 1968 to 1973. His Bachelor of Arts, Master of Arts, and Doctor of Philosophy degrees are all from the University of Chicago, where he was a student of the late Morton Dauwen Zabel, who first interested him in W. B. Yeats. His doctoral dissertation was on the literary theory of Yeats, and he went on to study AE, who was a close friend of Yeats. Dr. Davis is a member of the American Committee for Irish Studies and served as archivist and editor of the annual research report of the Committee from 1972 to 1976.

Other institutions where Dr. Davis has taught are Washington and Jefferson College (Pennsylvania), Heidelberg College (Ohio), Occidental College (Los Angeles), Parsons College (Iowa), and Midwestern College (Iowa). In addition to his specialty in Anglo-Irish Literature, he is interested in linguistics and the teaching of foreign languages.

Preface

AE died in 1935, and two years later John Eglinton published *A Memoir of AE*. For many years this book was the main source of biographical information about him. There had been some theses and dissertations written about AE, as well as numerous memoirs and reminiscences. But until 1975, when Henry Summerfield's detailed biography appeared under the title, *That Myriad-Minded Man*, we had nothing that even approached a definitive biography. This book was followed in 1976 by *George Russell (A.E.)*, in the Bucknell University's Irish Writers Series, written by Richard M. Kain and James H. O'Brien. In the meantime, Alan Denson had published in 1961 the bibliography, *Printed Writings by George Russell (AE)*, and *Letters from AE*. All of these books have greatly helped the student who wishes to know more about this very interesting and influential Irish writer.

My book on AE supplements the books mentioned above, and does not duplicate them. It is not a biography, and does not pretend to biographical completeness. It is rather a critical study of the major works of AE, with only as much biography as is needed to understand his works. Within the scope of this series, it seeks to do what all the books of this series do, to introduce the reader to the author and his major works. Since it is limited in space, it must also be limited in scope. I have included excerpts from the major works to illustrate AE's main concerns, concepts, and ideas. Although we have been promised a reissue of the major works of AE in the near future, at the time of this writing most of them are out of print and available only in university libraries. Thus these excerpts may be the only way the reader can experience AE's writings in their original form. It is my firm belief that literature should not only be discussed, but should be experienced.

AE was a versatile man, very eclectic in his sources. He did many things well, and wrote on a wide variety of subjects. His varied career led to the structure of the book. I could not have presented his work in strictly chronological order, as the result would have been complex and difficult to follow. Therefore, after the introductory biographical chapter, I chose to discuss each facet of his work in turn: his mystical beliefs and their expression, his poetry and other imaginative works, his economic ideas, his political theory, and finally his literary and social criticism.

Since AE was a mystic and since his transcendental ideas colored his entire life, the second chapter describes those books in which he develops his mystical visions and the mystical origin of his poetry. This chapter leads naturally to the third, which presents his poetry, its themes and techniques, and his development as a poet. The selections are chosen mainly from *Collected Poems* (1935), which contains, according to AE's own statement, his choice of his best poems. *The House of the Titans and Other Poems* (1934) was also included because it was not in *Collected Poems* of 1935 and therefore it completes the record. Some readers may find my treatment of AE's poetry incomplete and inadequate, but I have tried to give it the attention that is due in such a general work as this. Chapter four describes his other imaginative works in the genres of drama and fiction. His one play, *Deirdre*, is in my estimation a slight contribution, and his fiction had as its chief purpose the advancement of his mystical ideas and their application to the political and ethical problems of the time.

The fifth chapter turns to AE's economic thought, which reaches its zenith in *The National Being*, and shows the relation of his economic ideas to his concept of the Irish nation and its destiny, and to his metaphysical theories. In Chapter six, which follows from and is closely related to Chapter five, I consider AE's contribution to the struggle for Irish independence in the years between 1916 and 1922, his work with the Home Rule Convention of 1917, and his short, more or less journalistic writings related to the political problems of the time of "the Troubles." The seventh chapter brings the book to a close by reviewing his writings for *The Irish Statesman*, which he edited between 1923 and 1930; these writings were collected by Monk Gibbon in *The Living Torch* (1937) and are mainly in the fields of literary and social criticism, representing the mature thought of his final years. Some attention is also paid here to his painting.

This book would not have been possible in its present form without Alan Denson's bibliography and *Letters from AE;* certainly it would not have been as complete as it is. In 1964 I met Mr. Denson in England, and later we traveled through Ireland together in search of the sculptures of John Hughes. In the years that followed we became friends and colleagues in the study of AE. I am greatly indebted to him for his help and counsel, for his accurate and

Preface

patient scholarship, and for his careful reading of my manuscript. Without his help, the present book would have been much less accurate. Secondly, I would like to thank Dr. Sylvia Bowman for her careful editing of the manuscript.

The quest for material has taken me to the Reading Room of the British Museum, the National Library of Ireland, the Armagh County Museum in Northern Ireland, the Lilly Library at Indiana University, the Library of Colby College in Waterville, Maine, the Kenneth Spencer Research Library at the University of Kansas, the New York Public Library, and the libraries of the University of Chicago, Northwestern University, Harvard University, and Yale University. My gratitude to these institutions and to the persons who endowed them so liberally with Irish materials is immeasurable.

The list of other persons who have helped me would be very long, but I wish to mention in particular the help and hospitality of Mr. T. G. F. Paterson, formerly Curator of the Armagh County Museum, the present Curator, Mr. D. R. M. Weatherup, and Mr. Richard Cary, Curator of Rare Books and Manuscripts at Colby College. Miss Nina Meek prepared the manuscript for editing, and I appreciate her care and help. I think also at this time of the late Professor Morton Dauwen Zabel, who first interested me in W. B. Yeats and started me on the path which led to this book.

ROBERT BERNARD DAVIS

Tarkio College
Tarkio, Missouri

Acknowledgments

The author gratefully acknowledges use of copyright books and articles as indicated below:

To The *Atlantic Monthly*, for excerpts from "AE" by Diarmuid Russell. Copyright © 1943 © 1971 by the Atlantic Monthly Company, Boston, Mass.

To The Bodley Head, London, for an excerpt from *Protest in Arms*, by Edgar Holt, published by Coward-McCann, 1960.

To the *Colby Library Quarterly*, for an excerpt from "An Angelic Anarchist" by Oliver St. John Gogarty.

To Alan Denson, for an excerpt from "Reminiscences of AE" by M. J. Bonn in *Printed Writings by George W. Russell (AE)*, published by The Northwestern University Press, 1961. © Alan Denson 1961. Also for excerpts from *Letters from AE*, published by Abelard-Schuman, 1961. © Alan Denson 1961. Also for use of the picture of AE used on the jacket.

James Duffy and Company, Ltd., Dublin, Ireland, for an excerpt from *The Splendid Years* by Maire Nic Shiubhlaigh, 1955.

To Monk Gibbon, for Excerpts from *The Living Torch*, published by Macmillan and Company, Limited, London.

To the Macmillan Publishing Company, New York, for excerpts from *Innisfallen Fare Thee Well* by Sean O'Casey. Copyright 1949 by Sean O'Casey, renewed 1977 by Eileen O'Casey, Brehon O'Casey, and Shivaun O'Casey. Also for excerpts from *Some Impressions of My Elders* by St. John Ervine.

To the Macmillan Press Limited, Houndmills, Basingstoke, Hampshire, England for excerpts from *A Memoir of AE: George William Russell* by John Eglinton.

To Rowan and Littlefield, Totowa, N.J. for excerpts from the American Edition of *That Myriad-Minded Man* by Henry Summerfield.

To Colin Smythe Limited, publisher of the forthcoming Collected Edition of AE's works, for excerpts from the works of AE and from *That Myriad-Minded Man*. © 1975 Colin Smythe Limited.

To Henry Summerfield, for excerpts from *That Myriad-Minded Man*.

Chronology

1867   George William Russell born Lurgan, County Armagh, now Northern Ireland, April 10, to Thomas Elias Russell and Marianne Armstrong Russell.

1871   Enrolled in the Model School, Lurgan, until 1877.

1878   Moved to Dublin with family; attended Dr. Power's School.

1880   Attended Metropolitan School of Art, March to May.

1882   Enrolled in Rathmines School. Left in 1884 to study privately.

1883   Resumed evening classes at the Metropolitan School of Art, where he met W. B. Yeats.

1885   Left Metropolitan School and attended the Royal Hibernian Academy. Studied Theosophy and occultism with Charles Johnson.

1888   Attended meetings of the Dublin Lodge of the Theosophical Society. Began to write for journals, and first used "AE" as his spiritual pseudonym.

1890   Became a clerk at Pim Brothers, drapers, in Dublin. Worked here until 1897. Joined the Theosophical Society.

1891   Moved to home of Frederick Dick, where a group of theosophists formed a society, called "the Household." Lived here until 1898.

1892   Helped to found a theosophical journal, *The Irish Theosophist*, published from October 1892 to September 1897.

1894   Published his first volume of poems, *Homeward: Songs by the Way*. The Irish Agricultural Organization Society founded by Sir Horace Plunkett.

1895   Joined the Irish Literary Society in Dublin. Studied with J. M. Pryse, an American mystic. Met Violet North, who was to become his wife.

1897   Left Pim Brothers to become a bank organizer for the Irish Agricultural Organization Society. Wrote two pamphlets, *The Future of Ireland and the Awakening of the Fires* and *Ideals in Ireland: Priest or Hero?* Published second volume of poems, *The Earth Breath and Other Poems*. Mother died.

1898   Resigned from the Theosophical Society and revived the Hermetic Society. Served as president of the Hermetic

Society until 1933. Appointed Assistant Secretary of the Irish Agricultural Organization Society. Married Violet North.

The Internationalist founded with AE and H. A. W. Coryn as co-editors.

1899   First son born and died a month later.

1900   Second son, Brian Hartley Russell born. Father died.

1901   First and only play, *Deirdre*, published. A daughter born in July, died in August.

1902   *Deirdre* first performed. Third son, Diarmuid Conor Russell, born.

1903   Became vice-president of the Irish National Theatre Society. A volume of poems, *The Nuts of Knowledge*, published. The Macmillan Company became his publisher.

1904   Resigned as vice-president of the Irish National Theatre Society after a dispute with Yeats, who was president. Public exhibition of his paintings held. Published *The Divine Vision and Other Poems*. Edited *New Songs*, an anthology of poems by eight young poets published in this year.

1905   Appointed editor of *The Irish Homestead*, but continued for several years to supervise organization of cooperative banks. *The Mask of Apollo and Other Stories* published. Began his annual visits to Donegal in the summer.

1906   *By Still Waters*, a volume of poems, published. Also published *Some Irish Essays*. Moved to 17 Rathgar Avenue, where he lived until 1933.

1909   Published *The Hero in Man*, a pamphlet.

1910   Published *The Building Up of a Rural Civilization*, an address delivered to the annual meeting of the Irish Agricultural Organization Society. At the suggestion of AE, The United Irishwomen was founded.

1911   Published *The Renewal of Youth*, a collection of essays.

1912   Published *Co-operation and Nationality*, a guide for rural reformers.

1913   Supported strikers in the Dublin Strike; became a member of the Industrial Peace Committee, formed to settle the strike. Published the first edition of *Collected Poems*.

1914   Published *Oxford University and the Co-operative Movement*, a pamphlet.

1915   Published *Gods of War, with Other Poems*. Also published *Imaginations and Reveries*, a collection of articles reprinted from various journals.

1916   Published *The National Being: Some Thoughts on Irish Pol-ity*, his design for the development of an independent Ireland.

1917   Member of the Irish Home Rule Convention. *Thoughts for a Convention*, a pamphlet, resulted from this convention. Published *Salutation*, a poem commemorating the Easter Rising of 1916.

1918   Resigned from the Irish Home Rule Convention because he felt it was not effective in helping to solve the problem of Home Rule. Published *Conscription for Ireland: A Warning to England*, a pamphlet, and *The Candle of Vision*, a book describing his mystical experience.

1919   Published *Michael*, a poem of twelve pages, inspired by the Easter Rising.

1920   Published *A Plea for Justice*, a pamphlet demanding inquiry into attacks on Irish cooperative societies, and *The Economics of Ireland, and the Policy of the British Govern-ment*, a political pamphlet. His wife was afflicted with cancer and became an invalid for the rest of her life.

1921   Published two more pamphlets of Irish-English politics, *The inner and the Outer Ireland* and *Ireland and the Empire at the Court of Conscience*.

1922   Published *Ireland, Past and Future*, a pamphlet, and *The Interpreters*, an idealogical novel. Also wrote an "Open Letter to the Irish Republicans" for the *Irish Times*, an attempt to moderate the conflict over the Anglo-Irish Treaty.

1923   *The Irish Homestead* merged with *The Irish Statesman*, and AE became editor of the new *Irish Statesman*. Continued as editor until paper's demise in 1930.

1925   Published *Voices of the Stones*, a volume of poems.

1926   Visited Paris. His trusted assistant Susan Mitchell died, and his son Diarmuid joined the staff of *The Irish Statesman*.

1927   A libel action against *The Irish Statesman* almost caused bankruptcy.

1928   AE's first visit to the United States from January to March, followed by a second visit in June to receive an honorary Doctor of Letters degree from Yale University. Published *Midsummer Eve*, a volume of poems.

1929   *Dark Weeping*, a poem, was published. Received an honorary Doctor of Letters from Trinity College, Dublin. His son Diarmuid emigrated to the United States.

1930 *The Irish Statesman* was discontinued owing to financial difficulties. Visited the United States for the third time. Presented with eight hundred pounds by the Governor General of the Irish Free State as a token of esteem for his work for Ireland. *Enchantment and Other Poems* was published.

1931 Returned from the United States in May. Published *Vale and Other Poems.*

1932 His wife died at age 64. *Song and Its Fountains*, a description of the mystical origins of his poetry, published.

1933 Moved to London. *The Avatars*, a novel, published.

1934 Fourth visit to the United States. Published *The House of the Titans and Other Poems.*

1935 Returned to England suddenly because of illness. Died July 17 after surgery at Bournemouth. Buried in Mount Jerome Cemetery in Dublin. Awarded the Gregory Medal for distinction as a writer by the Irish Academy of Letters before his death. The AE Memorial Fund Committee established with W. B. Yeats as president. *Selected Poems* and a final volume of *Collected Poems* were published.

1936 *Some Passages from the Letters of AE to W. B. Yeats* published.

1937 *The Living Torch*, a collection of AE's contributions to *The Irish Statesman*, published by Monk Gibbon. *AE's Letters to Mínánlábáin* published by Lucy Kingsley Porter.

1961 *Letters from AE* and *Printed Writings by George W. Russell* edited and published by Alan Denson.

CHAPTER 1

The Man Known as AE

G EORGE William Russell, or "AE" as he was known, was a person of many interests and talents. Though he is not very well known in the United States today, he was one of the great men of his time in Ireland. Poet, painter, mystic, agricultural economist, organizer of cooperatives, newspaper editor, and good friend and protector of budding poets, this genial and kind man made a masterpiece of his life. At an early age he had charted his course: "I do not think I will ever try to get literary or artistic fame; art and literature do not interest me now, only one thing interests [me] and that is Life or Truth. I want to become rather than to know. If I raise myself I raise the rest of the world so much, and if I fail I drag others down also."[1] This modesty about his artistry is found in most of his writing, and it permeated his life, being anchored in his religious nature. Everything he wrote or said had the aim of improving himself and his fellow man, or of giving utterance to some noble idea. Since he did not concentrate his talents in the manner of Yeats or Joyce, his work in any one area may lack the high quality of the specialist; but taken collectively, his contribution was the fruit of a successful and distinguished life.

I *The Importance of AE*

It has been said that a journey to Ireland in the early part of this century was incomplete without a visit with AE. His broad interests, his fabulous memory, and his familiarity with the diverse sides of Irish life all made him an authority on Ireland. But because of his gentle and humble nature, it was not difficult to see AE and talk with him. In John Eglinton's firsthand account, written by a visitor to AE's home, AE is described as "the greatest Irishman of the present generation": "'I sat apart, waiting for Russell's voice, watching his every movement, trying in vain to capture his secret. All I saw was a kindly, humorous, wise man, of enormous tact and great toleration. If vanity is the womb of genius, then Russell has no genius. He is simple, he is courteous, he is free from pose, best of all he does not talk cleverly.'"[2] And yet, despite Russell's humility, he gave the immediate impression of greatness. As St. John Ervine said of him, "He fills a room immediately and unmistakably with the power of his personality."[3] Clifford Bax ranked him among the noblest men he had ever known, and this praise has been echoed by many of his friends and contemporaries. His son, Diarmuid, said that his father "possessed, more than any other person I have met, an air of spiritual power, an emanation of sweetness and tenderness that was almost as perceptible as the light from a lamp—and as hard to describe."[4]

Though Russell was born in Northern Ireland, he became one of the most powerful voices in the entire country. Neither Catholic nor Protestant, his inherent spirituality made him respected by many Catholics and Protestants. A nationalist, but not a revolutionary, his sincerity and objectivity in matters of politics caused him to be trusted by all parties, and by English statesmen as well. In the terrible days of the Anglo-Irish War he was one of those who pleaded for moderation and sanity. He was a leader of the Irish Renaissance, with great accomplishments in arts and letters, and was also a force in the development of the Irish cooperative movement, the cause sponsored by the Irish Agricultural Organization Society. As we read of him in the prime of his life, during the period from 1913 to 1923, it seems that he was everywhere at once, performing great deeds for his country and for the entire world. His great contemporary W. B. Yeats said of him: "He has the capacity beyond any man I have seen, to put with entire justice not only the thoughts but emotions of the most opposite parties and personalities—and men who hated each other must sometimes have been reconciled because each heard his enemy's arguments put into better words than his own."[5]

St. John Ervine said that AE and Sir Horace Plunkett, founder of the Irish Agricultural Organization Society, were two of the most important persons in Ireland, and that they were invariably mentioned in books written about Ireland in the period from 1902 to 1922.[6] John Eglinton stated that "AE was looked upon as a kind of 'key-personality' for his country's problems, and a visit to Ireland was not complete without an interview with him." He stated further, "There was no important intellectual or social movement on which he had not some authoritative comment, no important book with which he had not somehow made himself acquainted."[7] His faculty of rapid but exhaustive reading and his prodigious memory made him a good critic and an excellent conversationalist. C. P. Curran, a lifelong friend, has noted that his humility and kindness caused him to make no distinction between persons: "the latest and youngest new-comer had his attention as if he were the long awaited Avatar. The variety of his conversation was a Dublin proverb, ranging over philosophy, economics and the arts. The matter of his talk was copious and richly illustrated; his dialectic resourceful and dexterous; its temper beyond all praise. A kindly wisdom throned over debate, comprehending and all-forgiving. The most divergent opinions found patient hearing, but the immoderate appeared a little ridiculous."[8] In a country where writers are plentiful, where wit and good conversation are highly prized, AE was recognized as one of the leading minds of his day.

But above all, AE was recognized as one of the great spiritual forces of modern Ireland. He was an aphoristic writer, able to put great wisdom in a few words, and one of his favorite themes was that of spiritual development. He said that we become like that which we contemplate: "You become nobly like what you love and ignobly like what you hate."[9] As a student of the hidden wisdom of occultism, he practiced the golden rule of that discipline: "For every step you take in the pursuit of the hidden knowledge take three steps in the perfecting of your own character."[10] Katharine Tynan, a good friend of both Yeats and AE, and also a poet, said of him: "He is of the world, unworldly—the world's stain has never touched him; without religion, yet profoundly religious; the peace of God which passeth understanding lies all about him. . . . There is no room in him for any of the small meannesses of humanity. There is something strangely benign about him. He keeps his image of God undistorted, undefaced, as few of us have kept it."[11]

II *Physical Appearance and Personality*

In his mature years, AE was fairly tall, well-proportioned, but heavily built. Most of his life he wore a beard, his most prominent characteristic. Eglinton mentions his "tangle of mouse-colored hair," which he trimmed himself, his powerful head, his large full face with high cheekbones, and his blue-grey eyes. He spoke with an Ulster accent all his life, one that is difficult to describe, but

quite different from the accent that is usually described as Irish.[12]
He was indifferent to both food and clothing; James Stephens said
his overcoat looked "as if it had been put on with a shovel," and his
son Diarmuid quoted someone as saying "that he looked as if an
angel had come to earth and had seized the first human body it had
come across."[13]

Simone Téry, his French friend in later years, particularly commented on AE's eyes—grey-blue, tender, yet mischievous,
penetrating to the depths of one's soul. In addition, she said he was
poor because he chose poverty, putting his personal goodness and
the public good ahead of personal fortune and riches. He brought
out the best in people, and they turned to him instinctively. He was
a great talker, and in conversation he was humorous and amusing.[14]
At one point he said of himself, "I am always shocking my friends
by my low tastes, and I am grateful, for it relieves me of their in-
timacy and the trammels of respectability."[15]

His ability for rapid reading has been noted above, and apparently he had a photographic memory. He could recite any poem he had
ever written and claimed that if all his poems were destroyed he
could rewrite them from memory.[16] Diarmuid Russell describes how
he tested his father's memory one day: A book had been returned to
AE fifteen years after it had been borrowed. The book was out of
print, and it was not likely that AE had seen it since the time it had
been borrowed. When AE commented on the beauty of a particular
passage, Diarmuid asked him to quote it: "He repeated five pages
of prose with not more than two or three minor slips."[17] He could
tell time without a watch and tell people facts about themselves that
he could not possibly have learned in any usual manner. His powers
of concentration, perfected through long years of spiritual meditation, were also remarkable; he was frequently interrrupted in the
course of his daily work, and it was only through his great powers of
concentration that he was able to accomplish his duties as a
newspaper editor.

All of his powers came together in his intense spiritual nature.
One of his favorite quotations was from Stephen MacKenna's
translation of Plotinus:

Withdraw into yourself and look. And if you do not find yourself beautiful
yet, act as does the creator of a statue that is to be made beautiful: he cuts
away here, he smooths there, he makes this line lighter, this other purer,
until a lovely face has grown upon his work. So do you also: cut away all

that is excessive, straighten all that is crooked, bring light to all that is over-
cast, labour to make all one glow of beauty and never cease chiselling your
statue, until there shall shine out on you from it the godlike splendour of
virtue, until you shall see the perfect goodness surely established in the
stainless shrine.[18]

In this passage are fused all of the forces of AE's life, the complete
amalgamation of the moral, the spiritual, and the artistic ideals
which ruled his many-sided personality.

From all of these testimonials it might appear that AE was
perfect, but he would be the first to deny this. Though he was at
one time a vegetarian and was greatly opposed to the use of
alcoholic beverages, he smoked a pipe, but this was about his only
vice. He did on occasion become angry, and though he was gentle
he could strike hard. Oliver St. John Gogarty, physician and poet,
said that if there was any hatred at all in AE it was directed at two
entities, the "gombeen man," —Irish for the moneylenders who
preyed on Irish farmers—and the state. Both the gombeen man and
the state represented tyranny, which prevented the full spiritual
development of man.[19]

Above all, AE was a versatile man. He could have become great
in any of several areas, though he approached greatness in more
than one. He chose, however, to live life fully, leaving fame to the
specialists, believing that "A candle does not shine light in only one
direction." Diarmuid Russell said that this statement, so beautiful
in its simplicity, revealed to him the depths of his father's
character—how his father was more concerned with character than
with fame.[20] AE was a competent painter, a poet of great imagination and skill, an economist and a political expert, a critic of
literature and ideas, and a journalist. He was great in spite of
himself not as a result of his striving.

III   *Early Years and Family (1867 - 85)*

George William Russell was born in Lurgan, County Armagh, in
what is now Northern Ireland, on April 10, 1867. His father,
Thomas Elias Russell, was a bookkeeper, and there is no evidence
that he was interested in any of the artistic or spiritual ideas which
distinguished his son. His mother, Marianne Armstrong Russell, was
a native of Armagh. Both parents were members of the Church of
Ireland, but his father had evangelical leanings and attended the
Primitive Methodist Church. George was the youngest of three

children; a sister, Mary Elizabeth, died at the age of eighteen, and
his brother Thomas died a few years before AE. The family lived in
Lurgan for approximately the first ten years of George's life, moving to Dublin in 1878.[21] George continued to visit an aunt in Lurgan
after the move and for many years wrote to a friend there, Carrie
Rea; his letters to her provide us with much of our knowledge of
these early years.[22]

Russell attended school in Lurgan and Dublin from about the age
of four to the age of eighteen, attending a number of schools, moving more and more in the direction of art. He did not attend a university and seems to have been largely self-taught after his early
school years. He gave promise at an early age of being an artist, and
in 1880 and 1883 attended evening classes at the Metropolitan
School of Art in Dublin, where he met W. B. Yeats. Apparently he
also attended private schools in Dublin, one under the direction of a
Dr. Power and a second under a Dr. Benson, the Rathmines School.
Summerfield reports that although Russell later stated that he learned nothing at school, "being quite clever enough to evade
knowledge by seeming to possess it," he did win prizes in
mathematics, French, English, the classics, and handwriting. It
would be typical of him to deprecate his accomplishments in
school.[23]

In 1885 Russell transferred from the Metropolitan School of Art
to the Royal Hibernian Academy. This was his last experience with
institutional education, and soon after this he began a course of
private study through which he could develop his new interest in
spiritualism and occultism.

IV   *Spiritualism, Theosophy, and Business (1885 - 97)*

As a child Russell had walked in the country lanes around Lurgan
and had drawn the scenes that he saw. His spiritual union with
nature probably dates back to this time and these early experiences.
After moving to Dublin, he continued to visit an aunt in Armagh,
and later he visited the beautiful county of Donegal in northwestern
Ireland, where he painted many pictures of the Donegal landscapes
and seascapes. Thus the world of nature was always important to
him and forms the background of his spiritual development. At the
age of sixteen or seventeen, he says in *The Candle of Vision*, he
began to experience mystical visions, and these visions were of a
direct nature, antedating any influence of sacred books, acquain-
tances, or friends. As he had rejected the orthodox Protestant Chris-

tian religion of his parents at an early age, he was ready for the spiritual influences that were to inspire and shape his life and his career. Soon he met friends and read books which provided the intellectual base for his visionary experiences. The period from 1885 to 1897, when he joined the Irish Agricultural Organization Society, was devoted to mystical studies and to his efforts to earn a living.

His mystical experiences began in 1884, shortly before his meeting with Yeats, who was to be the first of his mystical influences. He began to experience "waking dreams of astonishing power and vividness," and he believed that these dreams came from a mind external to his own.[24] In 1885 he began the intellectual study of mysticism, and during the next twelve years he was influenced by a series of people and books, but always his strong personality controlled his beliefs, so that the totality which emerged was distinctly his own. The most important influence after Yeats, was Charles Johnston, who was converted to Theosophy in 1884 by A. P. Sinnett's book, *The Occult World.* Yeats had also been excited by Sinnett's second book, *Esoteric Buddhism.* In June 1885, Johnston founded the Hermetic Society, and Yeats was its first chairman. Russell remained outside the society, but he later founded another society of the same name in 1898.[25]

Other influences were Mohini Chatterjee, an Indian mystic who addressed the Hermetic Society in 1885; Madame Blavatsky, cofounder of the Theosophical Society; and James Pryse, an American mystic who helped AE develop a theory of Irish theosophy. Madame Blavatsky's *Isis Unveiled* was a strong influence on Russell, as were two books by Mabel Collins, *Light on the Path* and *The Idyll of the White Lotus.*[26] He was also acquainted with the *Upanishads* and the Bhagavadgita by the middle of 1887. Another book which influenced him was *Man: Fragments of Forgotten History* by two disciples or *chelas,* one of whom was Mohini Chatterjee.[27]

Russell joined the Theosophical Society in 1890, after two years of cautious observation of its activities, and remained a member until 1898. However, he found its discipline too strict, and after a dispute with the Corresponding Secretary, Mrs. Tingley, over an article he had written, and over other procedural questions such as the necessity for a hierarchy within the Society, Russell finally resigned. Soon he founded the new Hermetic Society, a loosely organized discussion group, which met weekly to discuss the writings of Madame Blavatsky and other theosophical scriptures. Russell was the president of this group until 1933, and it seemed to serve his needs more than the more tightly structured Theosophical Society. Though he remained a Theosophist all his life, his was an individual belief that did not follow any school. In fact, John Eglinton called him a "Protestant Theosophist."[28]

The Theosophical movement was part of the Spiritualist and Transcendental wave that was sweeping Europe and the United States during the latter half of the nineteenth century. A kind of reaction against the orthodox religions, Theosophy was derived largely from Eastern mysticism; but Russell and the Dublin mystics fused it with their interest in Celtic legend and folklore. Theosophists believed that spirit is immortal, that human souls pass through various incarnations, and further, that it is possible to communicate with the souls in the other world. It was not difficult for Russell, with the aid of Pryse, to devise a theory which related this belief to Irish legend. A new journal, *The Irish Theosophist*, was founded in October 1892, and in its pages, Russell and Pryse developed the theory that "the people of Cuchulain and the Tuatha de Danaan[29] had come to Ireland from an unnamed land which is clearly Atlantis, and they had brought with them spiritual powers to enrich their new home, a country destined to be the scene of a great revelation."[30] AE's article, "The Legends of Ancient Eire," published in *The Irish Theosophist* in March and April 1895, brought together the concepts of Theosophy and Irish legendary history.[31] The historical part was derived from Standish O'Grady's *History of Ireland*.

In 1888, Russell adopted his famous pseudonym, "AE." He had painted a series of pictures that depicted the development of man from his birth in the Divine Mind to his appearance on earth as the perfect man. Trying to think of a name for the series, Russell heard a voice say, "Call it the Birth of Aeon." Later, in the library at Leinster House, he found a book open and his eyes came to rest on the word, "Aeon," which he discovered was a word used by the Gnostics to represent the first created men. When he asked the librarian for information about the Gnostics, he was referred to Neander's *Church History*, in which he discovered "the myth of the proud Aeon who mirrored himself in chaos and became lord of our world."[32] For a time, he used AEON as his pseudonym; but when a compositor was unable to decipher his signature he printed it as "AE—?" Russell thereafter omitted the dash and the question mark and, adopting the first two letters, was known by them for the rest of his life. This cognomen summarized his main interest in life, identifying him with the spirit world and symbolizing the perfection of human nature.[33]

Apparently Russell was only employed irregularly until 1890, when he obtained a position with Pim Brothers, a drapery firm,[34] though Coates stated that he had worked for a time at the Guiness brewery. This seems unlikely, in view of his oposition to alcohol, and Summerfield's finding that he rejected a position which his father found for him at the Phoenix brewery.[35] During these years he was also writing poetry, and his first volume of poems appeared in 1894, entitled *Homeward: Songs by the Way*. From 1891 to 1898 he lived in a kind of a "commune" with a group of theosophists. Frederick Dick and his wife Annie rented a Georgian house in Upper Ely Street, near Stephen's Green, and invited members of the Theosophical Society to come and live with them. AE said that the seven years that he lived there were the happiest years of his life; it also marked a turning point in his life, as it was here that he met Violet North, an English girl who had come to Dublin in 1895 with J. M. Pryse. When they came to live with the members of "The Household," as it was called, they brought with them Madame Blavatsky's press. Pryse was a great influence on AE, as previously noted, and Violet North became Mrs. George William Russell in June, 1898.[36]

V   *Rural Reform, Journalism, and Drama (1897 - 1913)*

The years 1897 and 1898 saw a definite transition for AE, though it is difficult to mark another one for some time. He was married in 1898, raised a family, and became a leader of Irish life and thought in the years that followed. The year 1913 was chosen as the next transition because in that year, AE became interested and active in Irish politics, and the Dublin Strike of 1913 was the exciting force which caused this change. But actually, all of his life from 1897 to his retirement in 1930 was a single unit, devoted to many activities, both private and public.

In 1897 AE, as he was now known, published his second volume of poems, *The Earth Breath and Other Poems*, and two pamphlets in which he attacked the Catholic Church and offered Irishmen the alternative of a renewal of the ancient Gaelic heritage. In *The Future of Ireland and the Awakening of the Fires* and *Ideals in Ireland: Priest or Hero?*, he attempted to bring his new concept of Gaelic mysticism to the public and to convince his readers that the legends of Ireland would provide a more vital religious belief than would their orthodox Christian faith. But now he met Sir Horace Plunkett, who had organized the Irish Agricultural Organization Society in 1894, and Plunkett offered him a position as an organizer of rural cooperative banks. The aim of the Society was to develop cooperatives, including banks, dairies, and stores, which would enable the Irish farmer to become independent of profiteering moneylenders. AE's new task was to visit the rural districts and to organize banks. This work was more suitable to his interests, in that he now had a platform from which to speak, relating his mystical ideas to farmers and their basic rural occupation. To him, the soil was the source of life and it was divine; the farmers who tilled the soil were thus close to divinity, and AE helped them to realize their importance in the cosmic cycle of life. His new work took him to every county of Ireland, thus providing him with the rich knowledge of Ireland and Irish life which distinguished him and made him an authority.[37] In 1898 he became Assistant Secretary of the Irish Agricultural Organization Society, and though he continued to travel and address cooperatives, he was able to spend more time in Dublin with his wife and his growing family.

AE's new wife, Violet North, was a talented person in her own right. When J. M. Pryse left Dublin, she took his place as printer of *The Irish Theosophist*, to which she contributed articles under the name "Laon." She was also a visionary and very independent; for example, she smoked, when this was not usual for women. AE had struggled against his feeling for her, as he thought that romantic love and marriage were not consistent with his faith in Theosophy. But they were finally married and seemed well suited to each other, though they seemed to lead independent lives, AE concentrating on his many interests and his work, Mrs. Russell raising their two sons. After the birth and death of their first son in 1899, a second son, Brian, was born in 1900, and a third son, Diarmuid, followed in 1902. There was also a daughter, born in 1901, who only lived a month. AE's father died in 1897, and his mother in 1900.[38]

AE's son Diarmiud said of his father that he was not a domestic man, and it is not to be wondered at when we look at his activities in the years that followed his marriage. He continued as Assistant Secretary of the Irish Agricultural Organization Society until 1905, when he became editor of *The Irish Homestead*, a weekly which started as the official organ of the Irish Agricultural Organization Society. Though it later became independent, it continued to concentrate on rural affairs and cooperative news. Henry Summerfield describes the policies of H. F. Norman, AE's predecessor, whom AE succeeded as editor:

Besides drawing attention to co-operative developments abroad and engaging in polemics against the enemies of the movement, Norman campaigned for improved technical education, greater business honesty, more tillage and less grazing, and an insistence by farmers that both Unionist and Nationalist politicians pledge their support to co-operation. Especially prominent were his articles on the need to stem the emigration from the land by brightening rural life. Under his guidance the *Homestead* showed an obvious sympathy with the Gaelic League, which was reviving traditional arts and crafts in the countryside, and in November 1901 he promised that the paper would keep abreast of the [Irish] literary movement. New short stories by Irish writers and Gaelic poems with English translations were thenceforth a regular feature. There was no change in policy when Norman was succeeded by AE; the latter prosecuted with at least equal vigor every one of the campaigns that has been mentioned.[39]

AE also continued to write poetry, one play, several short stories, and an number of pamphlets, in addition to all of his writings for *The Irish Homestead*. Though he appears to have stopped painting from about 1890 to 1900, in 1904 Count Markiewicz persuaded him to join him and his wife, Constance Gore-Booth Markiewicz (who later became the famous "Red Countess" of the Easter Rising of 1916), in an exhibition of their paintings. This exhibition seems to have been the force that started him painting again. He continued to paint and to exhibit his paintings until 1915, and in August of each year he would vacation in Donegal, painting the luminous landscape of that beautiful county capturing on canvas its soft pastel shades.[40] Here he visited first the Hugh Law family at their home, Marble Hill, where on the hill behind the house was built for him a "fairy cottage," which provided him with a studio and a loft for sleeping. Later, when the Kingsley Porters rented Marble Hill, he stayed with them first at Marble Hill, then at Glenveagh Castle.[41]

In 1903, AE joined with W. B. Yeats, Maude Gonne, and Douglas Hyde to found the Irish National Theatre Society. Yeats was president and AE one of the vice-presidents. However, he resigned following a dispute with Yeats over the production of various plays.[42] Also in these years, AE began his practice of being "at home" on Sunday evenings to guests who would come to talk about literature and art. AE also was very helpful to beginning writers, and one observer, Maire Nic Shiubhlaigh, reported:

One discussed the work of new writers, analysed the work of established ones. Many a young man, introduced to literature in the Russell drawing-room, has since made his mark as a writer. Distinguished men of letters mingled with literary-minded clerks and shop assistants near the little fireplace and first manuscripts frequently changed hands for publication.[43]

Some of those young men, AE's "young canaries," as Yeats dubbed them, were Padraic Colum, James Stephens, Frank O'Connor, Sean O'Faolain, and Liam O'Flaherty—quite a distinguished group of songbirds. AE helped and encouraged them, but in no way did he attempt to impose his ideas upon them.[44]

VI   The Troubled Decade (1913 - 23)

Until 1913, AE had been known chiefly as an editor, a bank organizer, a mystic, a painter, a poet, and a writer on subjects related to agriculture and cooperation. But in the decade which began with the Dublin Strike of 1913, he achieved recognition as a national figure. He had predicted labor troubles in 1912, and his prophecy came true a year later, when the strike occurred; living conditions in the Dublin slums were disgraceful, and the reason was that wages were too low. The leaders on either side were James Larkin and William Martin Murphy. Larkin was the leader of labor, and Murphy was a wealthy man who controlled the trams in Dublin. On the morning of August 26, 1913, the drivers and con-ductors of the trams left their vehicles and walked home. The strike soon spread to other businesses, and four hundred employers joined in a lockout, which meant that the employers refused to negotiate or to permit their employees to work until they agreed to the terms set by the employers. AE joined the Industrial Peace Committee, which became the Civic League, and out of this emerged the Irish Citizen Army, which played a part in the Easter Rising of 1916. AE even designed a flag for the Irish Citizen Army.[45]

By October, the Dublin Strike had caused the lines between capital and labor to be firmly drawn, and AE aligned himself with labor. On October 7, the *Irish Times* published an open letter from AE denouncing the employers as "bad citizens, bad employers, and bad businessmen."[46] On October 28, James Larkin was convicted of sedition and sentenced to seven months in prison; AE came to his defense in an article published in the *Irish Worker,* and also by participating in a protest meeting at the Albert Hall in London. His article in the *Irish Worker,* with its rich irony, clearly showed his feelings for the deprived workers of Dublin. Of Larkin, he wrote:

He was preventing a sociological experiment of great importance to Ireland from being carried out. We have never accurately determined how little human beings can live on, and how little air space is necessary for families. . . . It is quite possible that after exhaustive experiments have been carried out . . . we might have found out that human beings could be packed comfortably in rooms like bees in a hive, and could generate heat to warm themselves by their very number without the necessity for coal. . . . Nothing is more annoying to scientific investigators than [the unscientific humanitarian—like] James Larkin, who comes along and upsets all calculations and destroys the labour of generations in the evolution of the underman, which was going along so well.[47]

The strike continued into 1914 without conclusive results, but it paved the way for the next great event of the troubled decade, the Easter Rising of 1916.

Meanwhile the Great War had begun in Europe, and AE published *Gods of War,* a volume of poems on the subject of war and its place in the life of the world-soul, in 1915.[48] AE was naturally distressed by the war and attempted to understand and explain this event as an aberration in the life of the world-soul. Meanwhile Home Rule had finally been passed by the British House of Commons, but the opposition of Northern Ireland and the coming of the Great War prevented it from being implemented. The Home Rule Bill was approved by King George V, but a Suspensory Act was passed simultaneously.[49] AE welcomed the concept of Home Rule, and his significant book of 1916, *The National Being,* was a design for an independent Irish nation based on many of AE's ideas of cooperation, economy, and politics.[50]

One of the most famous of Irish slogans is that "England's difficulty is Ireland's opportunity," and this proved to be true in 1916, when a band of dedicated Irish patriots willingly embraced martyrdom by staging a revolution on Easter Monday. The revolt was soon put down, and the sixteen leaders were executed a few at a time over a period of several days. To AE this was more than a public event. He knew three of the leaders personally—Padraic Pearse, James Connolly, and Thomas MacDonagh; and Constance Markiewicz, whose death sentence had been commuted because she was a woman, was his close friend. AE's exhibition of paintings with her and her husband has been noted earlier. Although AE did not comment publicly on the Rising, he regarded it as the inevitable result of the Dublin Strike and had predicted in 1913 some sort of trouble such as the Rising if popular demands were not recognized. His poem, *Salutation*, clearly indicates his sympathy with the cause and his admiration for the executed leaders.[51]

In 1917, the British government convened a Home Rule Convention to deal with this thorny problem, and it met for the first time on July 25, 1917. AE, along with Edward MacLysaght, was nominated by the government to represent the Nationalist point of view to compensate for the absence of Sinn Fein delegates, who refused to attend. AE's ideas about the convention are to be found in "Thoughts for a Convention," published in three installments in *The Irish Homestead*.[52] On February 1, 1918, he resigned because he felt the convention was ineffective and fruitless, because of the attitude of the British government and the failure of certain parties, notably Sinn Fein, to participate in the convention. Furthermore, the lines between the Unionists and the Nationalists had become so tightly drawn, that only one solution seemed possible, and that was the victory of Nationalism by any possible means. Also he felt that his continued membership in the convention would interfere with his work to further cooperation in Ireland.

All of these events were causing AE to become more nationalistic in his thinking and writing. The next development which aroused AE was the effort of the British government to conscript Irish men for the war in France. He opposed this action in a letter to the *Manchester Guardian* on May 10, 1918.[53] Conscription was delayed until autumn, and by that time the war was over, so that another political crisis was avoided. After the armistice, England again turned to the problem of Irish independence, and another home rule bill was introduced into the House of Commons. According to the provisions of this bill, Ireland would be partioned into Northern and Southern Ireland, each with its own parliament, with a Council of Ireland to consider matters of common interest to the two parts of Ireland. AE opposed this bill in an article written for the New York *Freeman*. Later the article was published as a pamphlet under the title, *The Economics of Ireland, and the Policy of the British Empire*.[54]

Meanwhile the violence predicted by AE was sweeping over Ireland. Some of the dairy cooperatives sponsored by the Irish

Agricultural Organization Society were destroyed by British police in retaliation against certain terrorist activities of the Irish Nationalists. AE vigorously attacked those responsible for the destruction of the creameries in an article written for *The Irish Homestead*. When the Chief Secretary for Ireland denied any responsibility on the part of the British auxiliaries for these attacks, AE called for his resignation. AE's demand for an inquiry into the destruction of the dairies was published as a pamphlet entitled *A Plea for Justice*. Apparently nothing came of his plea.[55]

The Anglo-Irish Treaty offered to Ireland in 1922 provided for the partition of Ireland and the establishment of an Irish Free State in the South, and a part of the United Kingdom to be called Northern Ireland in the North. This treaty was accepted by the Dail over the protests of the anti-Treaty party, later to be named the "Die-Hards" or "the Republicans." Those who supported the Treaty were called "Free-Staters." Although AE was opposed to the partition of Ireland, and clearly stated his position in his many journalistic writings of the time, he sided with the pro-Treaty forces, believing that the Treaty, imperfect as it was, would bring an end to the violence, and that it was at least a step toward Irish independence. His arguments for and against the Treaty are presented in a pamphlet entitled *Ireland and the Empire at the Court of Conscience*, published in 1921. His strong opposition to the violence of the Civil War and to the extreme position of the anti-Treaty party is stated in "An Open Letter to the Irish Republicans," in the *Irish Times* for December 27, 1922.[56] Whether or not this letter had any effect on the Republicans is not known, but peace finally came to Ireland, though it was the peace of a divided Ireland. AE predicted that a divided Ireland would lead to trouble in the future, and he was right. But it was the only solution available at the time.

VII *Last Years (1923 - 35)*

In 1923 the Civil War was over, the Treaty accepted, and AE was able to again turn his attention to journalism, poetry, and painting. The claims of Ireland had taken up much of his time in the ten years from 1913 to 1923, and much of his writing was of a political nature, devoted to moderating the claims of the extremists on either side of the struggle. *The Irish Homestead* merged with *The Irish Statesman* in 1923, with AE as editor of the new *Irish Statesman*, and the period from 1923 to 1930 was for him devoted to writing and editing that journal. Mrs. Russell, a victim of cancer, entered her last long illness in 1920, and until her death in 1932, was an invalid.

Until 1926, AE had traveled no farther than London. He had traveled to every county of Ireland in his work for the Irish Agricultural Organization Society, and probably no one knew Ireland better. In 1922, St. John Ervine wrote that AE had lived too long in Ireland and therefore lacked perspective:

I have wished at times [wrote Ervine] that "AE" could be removed from the atmosphere of adulation which envelops him in Dublin, and sent, without letters of introduction, on a tour around the world. He has probably travelled less than any other educated man in Ireland. He passes from his home in Rathmines, a suburb of Dublin, to the Office of the *Irish Homestead* in Merrion Square, from one center of adulation to another, with occasional visits to the home of James Stephens, where he meets the same people that visit him on Sunday nights, or to the Hermetic Society, where he meets them again.[57]

Ervine's hope was soon fulfilled. AE visited Paris in 1925; but more important, he visited the United States four times between 1928 and 1935. He did not need letters of introduction, for he was well known in the United States. But these four voyages did something for AE; they gave him what he described as "planetary consciousness."

AE's last years seem to have been lonely and filled with sadness. In 1927, a libel action against *The Irish Statesman* almost caused bankruptcy, and in spite of AE's efforts to raise money to save the paper by lecturing in America, it finally closed in 1930, and he went into retirement. Diarmuid emigrated to the United States in 1929, and Mrs. Russell died in 1932. But on the bright side, he began to receive recognition for his work on behalf of Ireland, the cooperative effort, and mankind: He received two honorary doctorates, one from Yale University in 1928, and one from Trinity College in 1929. Also, in 1930, he received a sum of eight hundred pounds, presented by the Governor General of Ireland, in recognition of his work for Ireland.

In 1933, he moved to London, feeling that his work in Ireland had been completed, and that perhaps a change of scene would help him to build a new life. But he was lonesome for Ireland and returned to Donegal for the last time in 1934. This visit was followed by his last voyage to the United States, which was terminated suddenly on account of illness. He returned to England, and died in Bournemouth in 1938, at the age of sixty-eight, in the company of his beloved friends, C. P. Curran, John Eglinton, and Oliver St. John Gogarty.[58]

AE was both spiritual and practical. The murals in his office, painted by him, symbolize the blend of the real and the spiritual in his life. Monk Gibbon described them: "AE's office, a room at the top of that building, seemed like an opening in fairy woods. He had painted each wall, from roof to floor, and there you looked on trees, and, beyond them, on beings rarely seen on land or sea, but always seen in the woods of vision and the air of dream. And there in the painted wood AE sat."[59] His long editorship of *The Irish Homestead* and *The Irish Statesman*, his work on behalf of the Irish Agricultural Organization Society, and his efforts on behalf of Ireland and Home Rule testify to his ability in the practical realm. His poetry and painting represent his work in the world of the spirit. This blend of the spiritual and the practical in his life was the result of his philosophy, which held that all things in the material world are governed ideally by the powers of the spiritual world. The wonder, said Clifford Bax, was that AE achieved any recognition at all in a world as materialistic and as agnostic as ours.

CHAPTER 2

The Mystic

A MAN of diverse talents and capabilities, Russell's belief in mysticism was basic to all of his activities. As a mystic, he claimed to have direct personal knowledge of the divine aspect of life that he derived from the spiritual world. This kind of knowledge goes beyond and behind the normal methods of knowledge, such as memory, testimony, authority, or even some types of revelation. For example, those who believe in Christianity derive their faith from the Bible; and this method of knowledge is called "revelation." The Truth was revealed to the writers of the various books of the Bible, and those who believe it accept their belief on faith in authority. The mystic goes beyond this kind of belief because his revelations of divine Truth are immediate and unquestionable.

As M. J. Bonn said of AE, "He lived in two worlds. In everyday life he was a practical man, but behind it he lived in a land of elves and of the little people whose language he understood and spoke. He did not create them by an act of will or stimulated imagination; they were *there* to greet him and he opened his house and heart to them. He and Horace [Sir Horace Plunkett] were near-saints, absolutely selfless."[1] AE would not discuss the grounds of his belief in visions; he experienced them, he believed in them, and the matter rested there. Furthermore, he believed that all men were capable of mystical experiences if they would but cultivate this inherent human ability by training and by belief. This capability was like muscles that had not been used or like a mental ability, such as speaking a foreign language, which had not been developed.

AE's mature mysticism should not be confused with the spiritualism or with the occultism which flourished at the end of the nineteenth century. Although some evidence exists that he and the Theosophists were interested in séances and in clairvoyance at one time, his inherent rationalism seems to have rid him of such interests. Instead, he became more interested in the spiritual forces that give life a deeper and richer meaning; and his mystical ideas might be summarized: first, he believed that the natural world is a living being filled with the spirit of life. The earth breath, as he called it, pervades all living things; but it is most accessible in the country, where it is divorced from the superficial coverings of civilization. He had the true romantic hatred of the city as being something corrupt and inimical to spiritual growth.

Second, AE believed that all human beings have access to the earth spirit and to the great memory which is the receptacle of all psychic experience. When someone dreams a dream, imagines something, or writes a poem, it does not die or fade away; all such experiences are stored in the great memory. Third, Druidic Ireland, with its legends of mythical heroes and its folk tales, is a local manifestation of this spiritual world. Other legendary cycles, those of India, Greece, or Germany, are related to the Irish system as parts of the great memory. In this way, AE's mysticism is related to his nationalism. Fourth, men today are in a fallen condition because they are unaware of the heroic souls that exist within them. They were once a part of the divine, but they have separated from it because they have become victims of the machine age, of the gombeen man, and of the city. Fifth, man can return to his ancestral self—to his pure being, "the uncorruptible spiritual atom"—in sleep, in dreams, and in vision.[2]

I *Early Works*

Three of AE's works that contain most of his ideas about mysticism are *The Hero in Man* (1909); *Renewal of Youth* (1911); and *The Candle of Vision* (1918); a fourth book, *Song and Its Fountains* (1932), describes the mystical origin of his poetry. *The Hero in Man* consists of three essays first published in 1897 in *The Internationalist* and *The Irish Theosophist;* the first of these essays begins by comparing the head of Christ with that of an outcast. Both are divine; inside the meanest of human beings is a divine nature, "the hero in man" which gives the book its title. Every man has this hero in him, whether he knows it or not; if he acts in an unheroic way it is simply because he is not aware of his powers. While the brighter divinities like Aphrodite and Apollo are prophetic of man's destiny, Christ and Prometheus reveal man in his present fallen condition, their sorrow mirroring his own; they help us to understand ourselves, and the reverence we pay to them must also be paid to every human being. "Christ is incarnate in all humanity. Prometheus is bound forever within us. They are the same."[3] Like Christ, all men are crucified divinities; and the meanest human being is therefore as holy as Christ.

The second essay tells us how to find the divine nature within us. Our deepest sense of this divinity comes to us when we are alone. Our sense of divinity leaves us when we are in the company of others, but when we are in solitude we become introspective and find that this divine world within us is peopled with many other spirits. When we write poems or stories they are not mere fictions, but are emanations from the spirit world. Since our divine natures meet in this spiritual world, we can influence one another; our duty as human beings is to find this heroic nature within us, to attempt to influence others through the spirit, and finally to attain seership. The last essay, which recounts some of AE's mystical experiences, is not always clear; sometimes it is rather verbose. In fact, his descriptions of his visions in these essays are not as clear as those in his later works, *The Candle of Vision* and *Song and Its Fountains*.

Renewal of Youth consists of essays which appeared in *The Irish Theosophist* between 1895 and 1897 and offers little that is new beyond the ideas described in *The Hero in Man*: for AE's main idea is that man is an outcast from the divine world; that he was divine at the dawn of the world; but that as time passed he drifted farther and farther from his divine nature. It is now necessary for man to renew his divinity, as the title, *Renewal of Youth*, suggests. The work reveals little progression of thought, merely emphasizing certain ideas in poetical and emotional language. His hortative and prophetic style is reminiscent of that of Thomas Carlyle: "I would raise this shrinking soul to a more universal acceptance. What! does it aspire to the All, and yet deny by its revolt and inner protest the justice of the Law!"[4] This kind of expression is typical of the Transcendental writer who, unable to ground his ideas in logic, resorts to emotional utterances.

Some of AE's new ideas not previously stated are that the soul transmigrates from body to body and from age to age, and that all the creatures of the world are linked together in a vast brotherhood, including both animate and inanimate nature. This belief seems to be similar to the eighteenth-century concept of the great Chain of Being described by Pope in *The Essay on Man*. AE says, "We believe in life universal, in a brotherhood which links the elements to man, and makes the glow-worm feel far off something of the rapture of the seraph hosts. . . . We are 'at league with the stones of the field!' " (9). This view leads to AE's ideas that the soil of Ireland is divine, to his love of the countryside, and to his frequent journeys to Donegal for renewal of his spiritual self.

To AE, who realizes the affinity of man with divine nature, nothing is evil; it merely *appears* evil to thoses who *are* evil. Referring to Tennyson's *In Memoriam*, where Tennyson speaks of nature as "red in tooth and claw," AE writes: "I do not believe in a nature red with tooth and claw. If indeed she appears so terrible to any it is because they themselves have armed her. Again, behind the anger of the Gods there is a love" (17). This Transcendental idea, which sees evil as a misapprehension of reality, differs from orthodox Christianity that sees man as prone to sin and error in his natural state but as redeemed by grace. Although the Transcendentalist sees man as good but in need of redemption, it considers him to be capable of this redemption if he will only seize his birthright. AE says in this respect, "We have imagined ourselves into littleness, darkness, and feebleness. We must imagine ourselves into greatness. 'If thou wilt not equal thyself to God thou canst not understand God. The like is only intelligible by the like' "(15).

II   *The Candle of Vision*

In 1918, when AE's longest book on mysticism, *The Candle of Vision*, was published, he took its title from two verses of the Bible which serves as epigraphs on the title page. The first is from Proverbs: "The spirit of man is the candle of the Lord," and the second comes from Job: "When his candle shined upon my head and by his light I walked through darkness." These two verses are central to AE's mystic belief and to the message of this book: Man has within himself a spiritual power by which he can illuminate his path through the darkened world of the modern machine age if he will only use it. The purpose of this book, therefore, was to examine in detail this spiritual power and to show the reader how he can use it; but *The Candle of Vision* also touches on many aspects of mysticism not covered in AE's earlier essays, including memory, imagination, sleep, dreams, intuition, legend, and myth.

The book begins with a reminiscence about his youth and about his first discovery of the spiritual life within himself. He had not always been close to nature; and, as a child, he had had no sense of the Wordsworthian identity with nature which we find in the "Ode to Intimations of Immortality." Not until AE was sixteen or seventeen had he become aware of the spirit within him:

I began to be astonished with myself, for, walking along country roads, intense and passionate imaginations of another world, of an interior nature began to overpower me. They were like strangers who suddenly enter a house, who brush aside the doorkeeper, and who will not be denied. Soon I knew they were the rightful owners and heirs of the house of the body, and the doorkeeper was only one who was for a time in charge, who had neglected his duty, and who had pretended to ownership. The boy who existed before was an alien. He hid himself when the pilgrim of eternity took up his abode in the dwelling. Yet, whenever the true owner was absent, the sly creature reappeared and boasted himself as master once more.[5]

"The boy who existed before" represents the animal nature; the doorkeeper, his conscious self; and the true owner, "the pilgrim of eternity,"[6] his spiritual nature. The spirit is the real owner of the body, not the animal nature which eats, drinks, and desires gratification of the appetites.

AE knew that his visions came from the great mother, "The Earth Breath," and he attributed them to her in one of his first poems:

> She is rapt in dreams divine.
> As her clouds of beauty pass
> On our glowing hearts they shine,
> Mirrored there as in a glass.
>
> Earth, whose dreams are we and they,
> With her deep heart's gladness fills
> All our human lips can say
> Or the dawn-fired singer trills.(6)

These visions of the divine were not continuous, for AE had times of doubt and vanity when no visions came to him. His first feeling was one of pride until he realized that the visions were not his own but were gifts from a superhuman source.

The third chapter, "The Slave of the Lamp," takes its title from a passage near the end of the chapter: "We have within us the Lamp of the World; and Nature, the genie, is Slave of the Lamp, and must fashion life about us as we fashion it within ourselves" (17 - 18). The Lamp is the consciousness of the divinity within ourselves, the "candle of vision"; and nature is the means by which the soul finds its true identity and worth. AE tells us how we may accompany him on the spiritual road to "The Many-Coloured Land" of spiritual awareness, for the journey is one any person can take, not requiring special gifts or genius. The method is simply meditation while, at the same time, fixating on an object: "I would choose some mental object, an abstraction of form, and strive to hold my mind fixed on it in unwavering concentration, so that not for a moment, not for an instant, would the concentration slacken. It is an exercise this, a training for higher adventures of the soul. It is no light labour. The ploughman's, cleaving the furrows, is easier by far. Five minutes of this effort will at first leave us trembling as at the close of a laborious day" (21). When we engage in this new labor, we arouse not only good spirits but also evil ones. Man's will, which is engaged here, is neither good nor bad but neutral; and it gives strength to good and evil spirits alike.

In "The Mingling of Natures," AE takes up a point which he raised in *The Hero in Man*: the idea that visions can be transferred from person to person. This idea is derived from Eastern mysticism, and it is also described by Yeats in his poetry and prose as the *anima mundi*, or soul of the world—a vast storehouse of psychic experience which contains all the thoughts and emotions of all persons who have lived since the beginning of the world. To the Transcendentalist, all thought is real and has existence; it can never be destroyed or lost; therefore, it must reside somewhere. This *anima mundi*, sometimes called by Yeats *spiritus mundi*,[7] is related to the One of Plato and to the Oversoul of Emerson; and, as AE describes it, it is "a memory greater than our own, the treasure-house of august memories in the innumerable being of Earth" (49). AE does not discriminate between Irish and non-Irish memories, for all myth derives from the great memory: "The beauty for which men perished is still shining; Helen is there in her Troy, and Deirdre wears the beauty which blasted the Red Branch" (61).[8]

AE had earlier distinguished between vision and imagination, and he discusses imagination in the *Candle of Vision* as higher and rarer than vision. Vision is like spiritual sight, a view from the windows of the soul; but imagination is active: it is the faculty by which the implicit is made real.

To AE, the imagination is an active creative force that results in pictures or expressions in language that did not previously have form or body; and his theory seems to coincide with that of Coleridge who describes the secondary imagination as a creative, shaping force in the thirteenth chapter of the *Biographia Literaria*. (The primary imagination for Coleridge is the act of the Creator creating the universe of which we are a part; therefore, the act of creation on the part of the artist echoes or imitates that of the Creator.) For AE the great memory contains all the psychic material of the ages, including myth and legend; the poet or painter draws his materials from this storehouse in the form of visions; and then, with his creative force known as the imagination, he bodies forth the poem or the painting. In this act of creation, the self reveals what it has derived from the great memory; and the self that recognizes this revelation is divided, therefore, into two parts: visionary and imaginative.

In the two chapters entitled "Dreams" and "The Architecture of Dreams," AE discusses the nature and origin of dreams. He is convinced that an intelligent being resides within each of us and that it remains awake while the body is asleep. As evidence, he cites the swiftness of dreams; for, since we could never imagine events so rapidly as they occur in dreams, an interior and transcendental force must be at work when we dream. Either dreams are self-created or they derive from some transcendental power; but, in either case, they develop from some cause beyond the normal powers of the waking person. In "The Architecture of Dreams," AE develops the idea that dreams have a conscious and intelligent origin in the subconscious, but he rejects the Freudian interpretation that dreams can be explained on the basis of suppressed desires or repression of the sexual drive.

The divergence between AE and Freud is the result of the difference in their insight and their purposes. Freud was interested in finding a cure for certain mental diseases; his insight indicated that if dreams were the latent material which correspond to our hidden drives and desires, they might give us clues as to the causes of mental illness. He was primarily a scientist, and his presupposition is that all phenomena must be explainable in terms of universal laws. To AE, interested as he was in creation and in the spirit, Freud's view was a mechanistic one that was an anathema; for his own world had to be controlled by intelligent forces which act spontaneously and purposefully. The two points of view are irreconcilable.

AE concludes that imaginations have body, existing in three dimensions instead of two. His feeling that he is able to control his imagination during artistic creation indicates to him that the creations of his imagination are three-dimensional ones. This example illustrates his meaning: "I imagine a group of white-robed Arabs standing on a sandy hillock and they seem of such a noble dignity that I desire to paint them. With a restlessness akin to that which makes a portrait-painter arrange and rearrange his sitter, until he gets the pose which satisfies him, I say to myself, 'I wish they would raise their arms above their heads,' and at the suggestion all the figures in my vision raise their hands as if in salutation of the dawn..." (106 - 07). To AE, it is amazing that these figures obey his will; and it indicates that they have not only bodies but minds as well; in other words, they are alive.

AE finds it much more difficult to believe that these imaginations just came together with no conscious will to guide them. A more convincing argument is that of the miracle of the acorn in becoming an oak, but it too is difficult to believe:

In that acorn which lies at my feet there is a tiny cell which has in it a memory of the oak from the begining of earth, and a power coiled in it which can beget from itself the full majestic being of the oak. From that tiny fountain by some miracle can spring another cell, and cell after cell will be born, will go on dividing, begetting, building up from each other unnumbered myriads of cells, all controlled by some mysterious power latent in the first, so that in an hundred years they will, obeying the plan of the tiny architect, have built up "the green-robed senators of mighty woods." (105 - 06)

AE implies that the only difference between the miracle of the oak that arises from the acorn and that of an intelligent being who sends us messages from another world is that we are accustomed to the first miracle but not to the second.

In a chapter entitled "Intuition," AE examines the inability of language to convey adequately the true sense of spiritual experience; and he concludes that something has been lost from the beginnings of life on earth when the first languages had a closer relationship to the experience which they were intended to mirror. Because there was a necessary connection between words and things, AE became convinced that there must have been a primitive speech which more clearly represented these spiritual intuitions; and he would have rejected the view of modern linguistics that all language is essentially arbitrary in its symbolization of things. AE's search for a primitive language which would relate more closely to intuitive spiritual experience leads him to the next chapter, "The

Language of the Gods." It is a strange chapter; and AE, who is clearly out of his element in it, admits that he lacks the knowledge necessary for this kind of study.

Leaving behind the subject of language, AE next discusses the idea of power. Since he has analyzed will, memory, imagination, and the other elements of spiritual experience, he now describes the idea of divine power without which we are helpless. This power comes from the will, and the will is more difficult to develop than either the intellect or a love of beauty. Persons who cultivate the will for the purpose of acquiring divine authority open the seal of cosmic power, and this act is dangerous if done for the wrong reason:

And indeed this rousing of the fire is full of peril; and woe to him who awakens it before he has purified his being into selflessness, for it will turn downward and vitalize his darker passions and awaken strange frenzies and inextinguishable desires. The turning earthward of that heaven-born power is the sin against the Holy Breath, for that fire which leaps upon us in the ecstasy of contemplation of Deity is the Holy Breath, the power which can carry us from Earth to Heaven. (140 - 41)

Since the will itself is neutral, it may be used for good or evil; the use depends upon the orientation of the individual who directs it. The power which is generated by the will takes different forms in different people. For AE, it took the form of visionary power, "the candle in the forehead," which he likens to Promethean fire.

The book concludes with four closely related chapters which take us into the world of Celtic mythology. In "The Memory of the Spirit," AE explains his visions as the memories of the spirit of man, one reincarnated many times in many ages. In other words, his visions are a form of "dreaming back," the words which Yeats uses to describe the act of the spirit in its rediscovery of those ancient and primitive archtypes of human experience. The spirit of man is eternal and has inhabited many ages in many parts of the world; its visions are memories of the many adventures of the spirit of man; and the ancient world depicted in Irish myth and legend is a form of this ancient heroic memory.

This idea leads us to the next chapter, "Celtic Cosmogony," which is not based on any textual authority but on AE's own visionary power. In this chapter, AE's Lir is the god of all creation, and he embraces everything that is to come. He is "an infinite being, neither spirit nor energy nor substance, but rather the spiritual form of these, in which all the divine powers, raised above themselves, exist in a mystic union or trance" (155). If this concept is difficult for us to understand, we should recognize that AE himself is not entirely clear as to Lir's nature; but he is possibly the spiritual source of all creation. Out of Lir came Mananan, the divine imagination and the root of all conscious life; from Lir came Dana, the Mother of the Gods, who represents Beauty and the spiritual form of matter. Later, she is referred to as the Mighty Mother or as Mother Nature.

The volume concludes by showing the relevance of the myths and legends of Ireland to Russell's view of his world. To him, it does not matter what names are used to identify the various persons in the Celtic cosmogony, for what is really important is "the vision of the universe" which underlies all of the mystic interpretations of life. To AE, the heroes of Celtic legend, the words of Socrates uttered through the writings of Plato, and the story of Christ are alike because they give us views of the spiritual world—a world which transcends the natural world in which we presently dwell. "Earth" refers to the spirit of the earth; to the concept that nature is alive, not dead; and to the idea that we can partake of the divinity of earth if we will only try to reclaim our lost birthright. Our religion has become abstract; we only go through the forms of religion; and we have lost contact with the real spirit of the world.

III   Song and Its Fountains

In *The Candle of Vision*, AE begins with mysticism, and proceeds to poetry. In *Song and Its Fountains*,[9] he works in a retrograde direction, moving from poetry to its origins in mysticism. His main idea is that poetry is written by a spirit within the poet's body. Throughout the book he refers to the marriage of inner and outer, the body and the soul, attempting to show how this inner spirit operates to produce poetry. The method is introspective and retrospective, as AE describes his first attempts to work backwards in time toward these origins:

I found, when I had made this desire for retrospect dominant in meditation, that an impulse had been communicated to everything in my nature to go back to origins. It became of myself as if one of those moving pictures we see in the theatres, where in a few moments a plant bursts into bud, leaf

and blossom, had been reversed and I had seen the blossom dwindling into
the bud. My moods began to hurry me back to their first fountains. To see
our lives over again is to have memories of two lives and intuitions of many
others, to discover powers we had not imagined in ourselves who were the
real doers of our deeds, to have the sense that a being, the psyche, was seeking incarnation in the body. (2 - 3)

The two lives are those of the body: the usual life that everyone
knows, with its superficial mental realm; and the life of the spirit,
which most persons never get to know because they do not follow
the method of meditation which AE prescribes. The many lives are
those of many spirits from time past and time present which continue to pour their spiritual essence into a man's own spiritual life.

The result of AE's retrospective method is the realization that
certain events of his past life had shaped his present spiritual life.
AE does not believe that we are born with a fully developed soul
but that it grows throughout life; and in this belief, he may be compared to Keats who outlined the development of the soul in his
letters. Three events in particular seem to AE to have had a great
effect on his later development as a poet. The first was his sensation
of beauty that was brought to him by the appearance of some daf-
fodils. Color was particularly important to him, and he even
remembers a story which fascinated him because of the hero's
sword with its blade of blue steel and its silver hilt (4). The love of
color had first seemed instinctive to him, only later did he realize
that the impulse came from a deeper life within him. The second
trait which came to him from his inner nature was his sympathy
with revolt, and he wrote at the age of fifteen, a violent passage on
behalf of those who had revolted against the orthodox religion of
Ireland. The third experience, the memory of a woman who lay dying and who wept because she could not nurse a sick neighbor, was
to AE another divine visitation which awoke in him the concept or
the trait of sympathy and of whatever was selfless in his nature.

As AE traced to their origins many of the desires and ideals of his
later life, he came to feel the presence of the spiritual being within
him—that of an entirely separate nature which attempted to inhabit
his body: "There grew up the vivid sense of a being within me seeking a foothold in the body, trying through intuition and vision to
create wisdom there, through poetry to impose its own music upon
speech, through action trying to create an ideal society, and I was
smitten with penitence because I had so often been opaque to these

impulses and in league with satyr or faun in myself for so many of my days" (8). We see here the duality in AE and in man: the animal life that is self-seeking, attempting to fulfill its animal appetites; and the spiritual life which derives its strength from *anima mundi*, writing poetry, creating art, and fulfilling itself in social action. He saw this governing myth not only in himself but also in others; he saw early in his life the origin in Yeats of the concept of self and anti-self. This concept ruled Yeats' life and is responsible for somuch of the duality in his poetry.

This inner being is, to AE, the author of his poetry; and, since a poem is "the most intricately organized form of thought," and since there is great intensity of consciousness in the creation of a poem, AE decided to try to trace the nature of the psyche in the origins of his own poetry. The result is one of the most precise formulations of the spiritual origins of poetry yet written. Whether or not we credit the divine origin of poetry as it is here described, and even though AE is not always consistent, his study remains one of the most searching ones of its kind. The essential idea presented is that in dreams the psyche splits into two parts, the *seer* and the *creator*. By *seer*, he means the part of the psyche that receives the dream; by *creator* the being who presents the dream (19). As in a motion picture theater where the audience views the picture, but did not create it, and is passive, so is the seer in dreams.

AE believes that poetry is born out of the interaction between the inner and the outer beings; that it is a form of inspiration which depends on our aspiration to a higher plane of mystical thought or experience. This view is the real meaning of his often repeated saying, "As is our aspiration, so is our inspiration." Because of this duality of the spirit, and because of the dependence of poetry on the inner spirit, AE says that there was always an element of the unexpected in his poetry: "I would be as surprised at the arising within me of words which in their combination seemed beautiful to me as I would have been if a water-lily had blossomed suddenly from the bottom of a tarn to make a shining on its dark surfaces" (24). Poetry comes chiefly from the waking dream, and, though most of us have had dreams in sleep and know what they are like, few of us have had experiences like those that AE here describes: "The waking dream may be likened to a living creature which invades us and obliterates all else in us until it has told its story" (25). Many of his poems derived from such waking dreams, and one

poem whose origin he describes may be compared with this passage
to show AE's method in the book:

In such a waking vision I passed out of an ancient city built by the sea. It
was steeped in the jewel glow and gloom of evening. There walked with me
a woman whose face I could not see, for my head was downcast and I was
rapt in my musing. It needed not that I should lift my eyes to see an image
that was burning in my heart. I had gone from body to soul in my brooding,
and the image was nigher to the inner eyes than it could ever be to the waking sight. We passed beyond the city gates, walking silently along the sands
to a distant headland. The sea and sand swept by my downcast eyes in fan-
tasmal flowings troubling not my thought. We came at last to the headland,
climbed up a little way and sat down, and still no word was spoken. The
love which was in my heart drew me inwards, and I was breaking through
one ring of being after another seeking for that innermost centre where
spirit could pass into spirit. But when the last gate was passed I was not in
that spirit I adored, but trembled on the verge of some infinite being; and
then consciousness was blinded and melted into unconsciousness, and I
came at last out of that trance feeling an outcast on the distant and desert
verge of things, though there was a cheek beside mine and I felt a wetness
and I did not know whether it was the dew of night or weeping. Then the
dream closed. (27 - 28)

When the dream departed, it left behind "Parting," "a slight lyric"
in which AE was unable to depict adequately the feeling of love
that had developed in the waking dream:

> As from our dream we died away
> Far off I felt the outer things,
> Your wind-blown tresses round me play,
> Your bosom's gentle murmurings.
>
> And far away our faces met
> As on the verge of the vast spheres,
> And in the night our cheeks were wet,
> I could not say with dew or tears.
>
> O gate by which I entered in!
> O face and hair! O lips and eyes!
> Through you again the world I win,
> How far away from paradise! (28 - 29)

The fact that he had not yet fallen in love led him to believe that
feelings first arise in the soul, and that external life later patterns
itself after our dreams.

The rest of *Song and Its Fountains* is an amplification of this idea of the mystic origin of poetry and of the concept of the duality of the psyche. AE believed that poetry could not be explained merely by reference to conscious experience and that, consequently, *The Road to Xanadu* by John Livingston Lowes is an inadequate explanation of the poetry of Coleridge: " . . . The logic of that analysis would almost lead to the assumption that when the palette is spread with colour it accounts for the masterpiece" (69). He seems certain that all great writers must have been the recipients of mystical experience and that they have then woven into their fictions the lives and the experiences of the many people who had lived before them.

The one example we have given of AE's description of the poem "Parting"[10] and its mysterious origin in vision is not sufficient; for only by reading the entire book can we master AE's certainty about the spiritual origin of his poetry. Admittedly, the mystical explanation is more interesting than the poem; moreover, we cannot take with entire seriousness AE's contention that all of his poetry developed in the mysterious way he describes. Although other explanations are possible and more probable, we get a sense of a strong awareness of spiritual power which influenced both AE's life and his poetry by reading the entire volume of *Song and Its Fountains* and *Collected Poems*. Toward the end of his book, he says that "Truth for us cannot be in statements of ultimates but in an uplifting of our being, in which we are raised above ourselves and know we are knocking at the door of the Household of Light. The poets and the great masters of music are those who have the expectation of inspiration. They wait upon the gods though they may not know when they turn inward in reverie what being it is upon whom they wait. They receive according to the quality of their desire" (91 - 92). For this sense—the power of inspiration which comes from the highest aspiration—we should read *Song and Its Fountains* and not necessarily for an explication of AE's poetry, though that too may come.[11]

CHAPTER 3

The Poet

I *AE's Poetry*

A E'S poetry, though limited in its scope, has been
highly regarded by many people; and John Eglinton tells of
persons who have been consoled, stimulated, and even saved from
death by his poems.[1] At first, Eglinton did not regard AE's poems
very highly; but the more he read them, the more he began to feel
their spiritual power. The admiration of James Cousins was even
less inhibited; he said that, upon first reading *Homeward: Songs by
the Way*, he "went on fire with the realization that immortal poetry
had been given to Ireland. Our own attempts at verse were as
nothing beside this voice that uttered from behind the curtain of
anonymity the most profound ideas and experiences in exquisite
verse."[2] Other readers have been more restrained in their praise;
but most have respected his verse. Ernest Boyd has summarized
AE's unique contribution to poetry but has also revealed his
limitation: "His songs have . . . a sensuous, unearthly note; they
do not speak of man's experiences in his normal unexalted state, but
of those rare moments of divine vision and intuition when his being
is dissolved in ecstatic communion with the Eternal."[3]

Some of AE's admirers have also criticized his verse. Monk Gibbon wrote: "He wrote no poem in which there was not beauty of
thought and sincerity of utterance, but he wrote many poems in
which the form seems inadequate and the imagery a little vague."[4]
To James Stephens, AE was limited by two characteristics: his
overuse of the same idiom throughout his life and the restriction of
his subject matter to the divine and theological. Nevertheless,
Stephens felt that AE was a great poet, and one of the two great
poets of the time;[5] and, although Stephens does not name him, the
other was probably Yeats. Clifford Bax, who compared AE to
Thomas Traherne, a seventeenth-century religious poet, mentioned
two serious defects in AE's verse: a lack of rhythmic subtlety and in-
appropriate meters.[6]

O'Casey's caricature of AE's verse, though exaggerated, is instructive. In the following excerpt from *Inishfallen Fare Thee Well*, AE's leading themes and his love of color are emphasized; one of the characters in the book, Edwin Droop Grey, calls his poems "a mass of glittering monotony." These poems are ". . . paralyzed with a purple glow. Swing-exultation in them all. They make a mind dizzy. It's too much of a thing to be friends with the Ancient of Days; too big a thing to be the rocker of infant suns; or to dip a forefinger into the fiery fountains of the stars; or to put on the mantelshelf of your room the Golden Urn into which all the glittering spray of planets fall. A.E. thinks he's God's own crooner."[7]

This criticism is difficult for the admirer of AE to accept, but there is a certain amount of truth in it—the same truth that we see in a caricature of someone we like and admire. AE *does* play too much on one note, and he does insist too much on his spiritual values. Likewise, the following caricature of his love of color has some truth in it: "Purple is his pride, and the one aspect in the mirror of the day is a purple twilight. There's hardly a poem of his left bare of the word Twilight, or of the color usually associated with that time of the day—purple mountains, lilac trees, violet skies, heliotrope clouds, and amethyst ancestral selfs."

The excellence and the limitation of AE's poems lie in the fact that he emphasized the spiritual aspect of life and that he injected into them the painter's love of color. His poetry was the embodiment of his religious feeling, and Ernest Boyd has rightly attributed this characteristic to an unconscious drive in him toward the religious: "It is the apparent absence of deliberate intention in the form and setting of the poems. The dusky valleys and twilight fields, the pictures which captivate the eye, are incidental, it might almost be said accidental. They occur merely as the accompaniment of an idea, the prelude to a statement which constitutes the real reason of the poem's existence."[8] For the most part, AE's poetry must be accepted and evaluated as religious poetry. As Abinash Chandra Bose has said, AE's is "the poetry of spiritual exaltation, in which the soul soars to heights unknown to the ordinary consciousness."[9]

AE's letters to Charles Weekes reveal that most of his poems were composed in the open air.[10] It was apparently necessary for him to establish direct and immediate contact with nature in order to achieve his artistic purpose. Though thought was important in his poetry, he did not write with the thought or the philosophy in mind. The intuitive feeling for nature came first, and the philosophical implications came later. "The Great Breath," for example, was written while he was watching a beautiful twilight; and he later discovered its relationship to Hegel's philosophy. He said, "I always attach more importance to the intuition or vision than to the after interpretations which I almost always make myself."[11]

AE has been compared with Algernon Charles Swinburne for his poetical skill, and with Ralph Waldo Emerson and William Blake for his thought. The comparison to Blake is quite apt since both were visionaries and since both were visual artists as well as poets. There is evidence that AE was very familiar with both Blake's writings and his drawings,[12] but AE greatly resembles another poet-painter, Dante Gabriel Rossetti, in his love of color and in his willingness to sacrifice ideas or sense to the sounds and colors of poetry. But, of course, the poet with whom AE is most often compared is his friend Yeats. Eglinton, who has called the two poets the *Dichterpaar* of modern Irish poetry, has indicated that Yeats had the greater poetic endowment and the wider worldly experience but that his range of abilities and activity was narrower than that of AE.[13] Diarmuid Russell has said that his father readily acknowledged Yeats to be the better poet; for, as AE explained, "Willie is a much better poet than I am. He is a great poet. He devotes all his time to his art and can spend days reworking a line or a verse till it has reached his ultimate in perfection. I, on the other hand, have to do many, many things, some by desire and some by compulsion."[14] They were also different in their reactions to mystical ideas; for, while AE accepted the mystical ideas that he encountered, and made them a part of his life, for Yeats they were only the material for his poetry.[15]

II   Themes and Techniques

The introductory note of the 1935 edition of *Collected Poems* indicates that the majority of the poems in that volume were collected from *Homeward: Songs by the Way* (1894), *The Earth Breath* (1897), *The Divine Vision* (1904), and *Voices of the Stones* (1925); that certain new verses were included, and that the collection contained all the poetry that AE wished his friends to read. AE explained his principle of selection: "I have omitted what in colder hours seemed to me to have failed to preserve some heat of the imagination; but in that colder mood I have made but slight revision of those retained. However imperfect they seemed, I did not feel

that I could in after hours melt and remould and make perfect the
form if I was unable to do so in the intensity of conception, when I
was in those heavens we breathe for a moment and then find they
are not for our clay."[16] With such a statement from the author, it
seems logical to use the 1935 edition of the *Collected Poems* as the
corpus for a study of AE's poetry. All numbers in parentheses refer
to this volume. One additional volume, *The House of the Titans
and Other Poems* (1934) is included, however, because it contains
important poems not appearing in *Collected Poems.*

The lack of variety in AE's poetry has been noted by his friends
and his critics; his favorite verse form is the four-line ballad stanza,
and most of his poems are about nature and the mystery behind it.
Poem after poem describes the mighty being who stands myste-
riously behind his creations. His poetry is full of color, not just
violet and purple but with many others; and "The Great Breath" is
an example of this profusion of color:

> Its edges foamed with amethyst and rose,
> Withers once more the old blue flower of day:
> There where the ether like a diamond glows
>   Its petals fade away.
>
> A shadowy tumult stirs the dusky air;
> Sparkle the delicate dews, the distant snows;
> The great deep thrills, for through it everywhere
>   The breath of Beauty blows.
>
> I saw how all the trembling ages past,
> Moulded to her by deep and deeper breath,
> Neared to the hour when Beauty breathes her last
>   And knows herself in death. (9)

We also see here certain other characteristics of his early verse: the
painter's eye for color and the vagueness of meaning where sense is
sacrified to music. Both of these characteristics identify him with
Rossetti. The lines are not sharp but hazy and suggestive—a style
which would be called "painterly" in the visual arts. The inverted
sentence structure, as in "Sparkle the delicate dews," marks him as
a nineteenth-century poet; Robert Browning reveals the same style
in "Rabbi Ben Ezra," with the line "Irks care the cropful bird?"
What thought emerges is also typical of AE and the tradition of
Romanticism: the mystery of nature, its beauty, its divinity, and its

fragility. The difficulty in this poem comes in the final line where
AE seems to be saying that Beauty must die; yet Beauty is also identified with "The Great Breath," which is a kind of divinity in Nature. If she is eternal, then why must she die? This kind of confu-
sion is typical of the early AE, who did not sufficiently rework his
material.

We see the same tendencies in "The Divine Vision," plus certain
other characteristics of AE's verse, including the use of such archaic
diction as *thee, thy, thou, ope, seest.* The theme is the human soul
in exile, another typical theme for AE. In "A Vision of Beauty," we
see his vision as he watches the sky at dawn and as the veil is lifted
for him:

> Many coloured shine the vapours: to the
>   moon-eye far away
> 'Tis the fairy ring of twilight, mid the spheres
>   of night and day,
> Girdling with a rainbow cincture round the
>   planet where we go,
> We and it together fleeting, poised upon the
>   pearly glow;
> We and it and all together flashing through
>   the starry spaces
> In a tempest dream of beauty lighting up the
>   face of faces. (86 - 87)

The difficulty of our analyzing such poetry can be readily seen, and
our problem is the same one we have with Rossetti's *The House of
Life* and with some of the more symbolic poetry of Yeats; for
thought in such poetry is sacrificed for music and image.

We also find the world-weary quality in much of AE's poetry that
is evident in that of the early Yeats, and, though Yeats outgrew this
mood, it remained with AE to the end of his career. The poems
which reveal this world-weariness reflect the idea that the world has
degenerated from the freshness of the Golden Age and that man has
fallen from his ancestral greatness. This feeling is evident in the
final stanza of AE's poem called "Weariness:"

> And I yearn to lay my head
> Where the grass is green and sweet,
> Mother, all the dreams are fled
> From the tired child at thy feet. (182)

It is also evident in "Carrowmore," an earlier poem reminiscent of Yeats's "The Stolen Child"; and even AE's meter is similar:

> "Come away," the red lips whisper, "all the
>   world is weary now;
> 'Tis the Twilight of the ages and it's time to
>   quit the plough.
> Oh, the very sunlight's weary ere it lightens
>   up the dew,
> And its gold is changed and faded before it
>   falls to you." (106 - 07)

That AE never outgrew this mood is recorded in a few lines that are found in one of his last poems, "A Farewell":

> Exiled, we pine for the King in His beauty.
>   We long for the day
> When this shadow show shall be over, the
>   masks we wore thrown away—
> The monstrous masks that veiled us, of satyr,
>   demon and faun—
> And be lovely, starry and ancient with youth
>   as we were in the dawn. (412)

As we have noted, the majority of AE's poems in the *Collected Poems* volume of 1935 serve as vehicles for his mystic philosophy, and the first group of poems to be described is concerned with the nature of God. These poems include "Oversoul" (8), "The Unknown God" (5), "By the Margin of the Great Deep" (3), and "The Twilight of Earth" (183 - 85). The supreme deity, as differentiated from the Divine Mother who appears in some of the poems, is always designated as a male god; but AE does not know much about him. Mysterious and ineffable, he is known chiefly through his creation, the world of nature. The title of the poem, "Oversoul," is from Emerson, and the epigraph is from the Bhagavadgita: "I am Beauty itself among beautiful things." Although AE's god is found in the beautiful things of nature, the poet is not at all certain of his location or of the source of divine beauty:

> The flame of Beauty far in space—
> Where rose the fire: in Thee? in Me?
> Which bowed the elemental race
> To adoration silently? (8)

Questions are raised, but no answers are given. "The Unknown
God" is the title of the second poem, and even the title conveys a
sense of ignorance about God's nature or location. What it adds is
the idea of spiritual intoxication: "Our hearts were drunk with a
beauty/Our eyes could never see" (5). AE usually experiences God
at the close of day or at dawn. In "By the Margin of the Great
Deep," the time is twilight, AE's favorite time of day; "the great
deep" does not refer to the sea but to the sky, or possibly to a
metaphorical ocean similar to Wordsworth's "immortal sea that
brought us hither" in the "Ode to Intimations of Immortality."

Sometimes the beauty and glory of God are symbolized by his
creatures, by a tree in "Rest" (28), or by the stars in "Star
Teachers" (15). In "Rest," a tree that personifies nature speaks to a
bird, which represents man, and tells it to be free and not to depend
too much on the tree. But, when the bird is tired, the tree will wrap
it in its loving leaves. The lesson for man is clear: do not depend too
much on comforts and safety, but be free and enjoy life. In "Star
Teachers," the stars are man's instructors, helping him to find God:

> These myriad eyes that look on me are mine;
> Wandering beneath them I have found again
> The ancient ample moment, the divine,
>   The God-root within men. (15)

Two of AE's favorite words are *myriad* and *God-root*. The latter expression implies that there is a divine root in all men, but the leaves
are sometimes withered. If we can find that root, the "uncorrupted
spiritual atom," then it is possible to make man religious again.

In "Symbolism" (47 - 48), AE sees all the natural objects of the
earth as symbols of the higher spiritual life. The fires in the cottages
are compared to the lights from the stars, and the final stanza sums
up the idea that we are carried to God by these divinely inspired
symbols:

> Nearer to Thee, not by delusion led,
> Though there no house fires burn nor bright eyes gaze:
> We rise, but by the symbol charioted,
> Through loved things rising up to Love's own ways:
> By these the soul unto the vast has wings
> And sets the seal celestial on all mortal things. (48)

In some of the poems, such as "The Virgin Mother" (35 - 36) and
"Dana" (37 - 38), the divinity is a goddess; but she seems to be a

personification of the earth spirit and is subordinate to God, the creator. The earth is divine—even the soil, the dust, and the dirt are to be worshiped, as he makes clear in "Dust":

> I heard them in their sadness say,
> "The earth rebukes the thought of God;
> We are but embers wrapped in clay
> A little nobler than the sod."
>
> But I have touched the lips of clay,
> Mother, thy rudest sod to me
> Is thrilled with fire of hidden day,
> And haunted by all mystery. (34)

In "The Virgin Mother," he develops the same paradox: All of the noble queens of history, the lover's heart, and the lips of the beloved were born "Within that dark divinity of earth,/Within that mother being you despise" (35).

Dana, AE says in a note at the end of *Collected Poems*, is the "Hibernian mother of the gods who were named from her Tuatha De Danaan, or the Tribes of the goddess Dana. They are also sometimes called the Sidhe [pronounced *shee*]" (428). In the poem bearing her name, she is the speaker; and she tells us that she is the spirit of love, the feminine element in life, the provider of comfort and solace, and the one who counterbalances the male destructive element in life:

> I breathe
> A deeper pity than all love, myself
> Mother of all, but without hands to heal:
> Too vast and vague, they know me not.
>   But yet,
> I am the heartbreak over fallen things,
> The sudden gentleness that stays the blow,
> And I am in the kiss that foemen give
> Pausing in battle, and in the tears that fall
> Over the vanquished foe. . . . (38)

She might be compared to the Germanic Hertha, who is celebrated by Swinburne in the poem bearing that name. She is also Mother Nature and is identified with Ireland, whose soil is divine. This spirit is female, obviously because of the fact that the earth is fertile, identifying with fertility in women.

Because of all this divinity which surrounds him, what to AE is

the position of man? Is he, too, divine? He *was* divine; he would be
divine again if only he knew of his divine origin. In another group
of poems, AE treats the fallen nature of man. Some of these poems
are "The Robing of the King" (215 - 17), "Faith" (275), "The
Twilight of Earth" (183 - 85), and "Children of Lir" (160 - 61). In
"The Robing of the King," a poem full of rich imagery, the king is
the "ancestral self"—that divine first man who lived before the fall
and who symbolizes the spiritual plane which man can attain if he
will contemplate the beautiful and the spiritual. He is also a Christ
figure:

> Fire, an aureole encircling, suns his brow with gold,
> Like to one who hails the morning on the mountains old.
> Open mightier vistas, changing human loves to scorns,
> And the spears of glory pierce him like a crown of thorns. (216)

This very rich symbolic poem telescopes the ideas of the divinity of
man, the divinity of Christ, and the fallen nature of man which is
represented by the crucifixion of Christ. In "Faith" (275), AE
accepts the fallen nature of man from Christian doctrine when he
admits that "We took forbidden fruit and ate/Far in the garden of
His mind." But he rejects the idea that God wants man to debase
himself; He is kind and wants man to realize his own goodness: "He
does not love the bended knees,/The soul made wormlike in His
sight. . . ."

The fallen nature of man, the divinity of earth, and Celtic legend
are all brought together in a group of poems bearing the titles "The
Twilight of Earth" (183 - 85), "Children of Lir" (160 - 61), "A Call
of the Sidhe" (218 - 19), "The House of the Titans"[17] and "The
Nuts of Knowledge" (158 - 59). The legendary references in these
poems are clarified in the notes at the end of *Collected Poems*. The
ideas found in all of these poems are brought to a focus in "The
Twilight of Earth" which describes the early days of legend when
the earth was fresh and new and which contrasts that world with the
present aged and materialistic one that is now in its twilight.

> The wonder of the world is o'er:
>   The magic from the sea is gone:
> There is no unimagined shore,
>   No islet yet to venture on.
> The Sacred Hazels' blooms are shed,
> The Nuts of Knowledge harvested. (183)[18]

Can we not return to our primeval power, turning back the calendar to those early days when the world was pure and man was good? We can if only we will it:

> The power is ours to make or mar
>   Our fate as on the earliest morn,
> The Darkness and the Radiance are
>   Creatures within the spirit born. (184)

"Children of Lir" tells essentially the same story; for in this poem the children of Lir, the Oceanus of Celtic mythology and the source of all life, come to the earth in the form of swans and express their desire to return to "the infinite Lir." The lilting music of the anapests make this one of the loveliest of AE's poems. This poem concludes:

> Still gay is the breath in our being, we wait
>   for the bell branch to ring
> To call us away to the Father, and then we
>   will rise on the wing,
> And fly through the twilights of time till the
>   home lights of heaven appear;
> Our spirits through love and through longing
>   made one in the infinite Lir. (161)

The story is repeated in "A Call of the Sidhe" in which the tribes of Dana, the ancient people of the wind, are depicted as calling to the human world and is tempting it to return to the spirit. In "The House of the Titans," a long narrative poem based on the myth of the Children of Lir, AE describes the fall of man into the physical world and away from the ancestral lights. Nuada, king of the Titans,[19] is the central figure who dreams of the past splendor of his life in the spirit world.

Sometimes AE relates his typical themes to Indian mythology and religion, as in "Krishna" (61 - 62). Krishna was one of the many incarnations of Vishnu; and since he had the peculiar ability to appear in many different forms, he was by turns a naughty and mischievous child, an amorous adolescent known for his many love affairs, and a warrior. In this poem, AE depicts Krishna as a child, a lover, a drunken outcast, the Prince of Peace, a horrible monster, the Light of Lights, a miser, and a prodigal. In other words, Krishna represents all of the contrary characteristics that can comprise the human personality. In this poem, one of AE's best, he describes the human condition by pointing to the divinity in man and by contrasting that with his depravity.

In "The Heroes" (79 - 81), another poem about the latent divinity in man, AE is walking in the city, dejected by all the corruption he sees. A man approaches who seems to be a Christ figure, and he shows AE the more lovely aspects of the city. In a long speech—a rather improbable one from a mere chance acquaintance in the street—the man says that the lost and fallen people we see in the street will pass into the divine world when they sleep tonight. They have divinity within them:

> "As bright a crown as this was theirs when first
>   they from the Father sped;   .
> Yet look with deeper eyes and still the ancient
>   beauty is not dead." (80)

AE is constantly asking us to look with deeper eyes through the surfaces of life, penetrating to the divine within man and nature. The man fades into the crowd, but the poet now sees with new eyes:

> He mingled with the multitude. I saw their
>   brows were crowned and bright,
> A light around the shadowy heads, a shadow
>   round the head of light. (81)

"Germinal" (400 - 01), one of AE's later poems, is in the same vein; for the title refers to the early stage of the development of man and his divine origin. This poem shows, however, greater firmness and has more intensity than the early poem because it is developed chiefly through allusions to other materials, has a sense of paradox, and contains freshness and intensity of thought. Here he refers to Dante's love for Beatrice:

> All the strong powers of Dante were bowed
>   To a child's mild eyes,
> That wrought within him that travail
>   From depths up to skies,
> Inferno, Purgatorio
> And Paradise. (400 - 01)

The idea presented in this stanza is that goodness and gentleness prevail over power and strength, but the poet shows in another stanza the power of a child in a different and novel way:

> In ancient shadows and twilights
> > Where childhood had strayed,
> The world's great sorrows were born
> > And its heroes were made.
> In the lost boyhood of Judas
> > Christ was betrayed. (401)

AE seems to be saying that the effect of an act can never be foretold and that even the gentlest forces have far-reaching consequences: Beatrice influenced Dante to write the *Divine Comedy,* and the boy Judas had already within him the traits which led to the betrayal of Christ. Whatever our destiny, we must live our lives to the end and accept the ultimate divinity in man.

Another group of poems describes the blessedness of children and childhood: "Awakening" (2), "Childhood" (45), "The Dream of the Children" (108 - 10), and "Om" (155 - 56). The basic idea in these poems is the usual primitivist concept that children, being closer to God, are more blessed than adults. In "Childhood," the poet contrasts with the adult world of care, strife, and duty the divinely inspired life of the child. In this respect, AE is similar to Wordsworth in his belief about the unconscious divinity of children that is revealed in such poems as the sonnet, "It Is a Beauteous Evening" or the "Intimations" ode. To AE, men learn only from pain and sorrow, but an inner joy guides the child:

> We are men by anguish taught
> To distinguish false from true;
> Higher wisdom we have not;
> But a joy within guides you. (45)

"Om" refers to the sacred word in Hinduism which has magic properties, a prayer in a single word, supposedly spoken by Brahma himself. In this poem in which a child says the sacred word and is united with Brahma, the simplicity of the style is somewhat reminiscent of that of Blake:

> And here the voice of earth was stilled,
> The child was lifted to the Wise:
> A strange delight his spirit filled,
> And Brahm looked from his shining eyes. (156)

Just as this poem deals with the true view of life, "The Veils of Maya" (126) is concerned with the false view. *Maya,* which means "illusion," is one of the ideas of Eastern mysticism that life is filled with illusions which must be penetrated to find the divine.

Two poems about the materialism of the modern world, dominated as it is by machinery and urbanization, are "The Iron Age" (267 - 69) and "The Iron Age Departs."[20] The first of these is very critical of modern politics and economics. Once our leaders were gods, but now "We choose the chieftains of our race/From hucksters in the market place" (267). In modern times we seem to worship the devil instead of the highest gods, and AE asks "Have all the gods their cycles run?/Has devil worship now begun?" (267). The answer seems to be in the affirmative, for man's values fall when he finds that life is not so precious as death. The events since 1934 would probably convince AE that he was right when he wrote these lines:

> O whether devil planned or no,
> Life here is ambushed, this our fate,
> That road to anarchy doth go,
> This to the grim mechanic state.
> The gates of hell are open wide,
> But lead to other hells outside. (267 - 68)

He concludes that we need a new savior, "the iron age's avatar." The second poem, "The Iron Age Departs," describes a pair of lovers who find joy in an innocent love, that is stripped of all physical desire. This idea leads the poet into a dream of the Golden Age when the world will again be peaceful and harmonious as it was before the Fall. But the dream cannot last, for he is awakened by the "dragon croak of the city."

AE's attitude toward the city is revealed in a group of poems including "Pity" (29), "The City" (30 - 33), "Michael" (358 - 69), "New York" (414), and "In A Strange City" (418 - 19). His distrust of the city is typically Romantic, and it is based on the primitivistic idea that man is good by nature but corrupted by civilization—an idea which goes back to Rousseau. But AE's attitude toward the city is ambivalent: in "Pity," he sees it as evil; in "The City," he sees possibilities of spiritual values. The epigraph to "The City" reads "Full of Zeus the cities: full of Zeus the harbors: full of Zeus are all the ways of men." God is everywhere, even in the city, if we can find Him. As AE walks through Dublin, he sees people and objects, all of whom have spiritual possibilities; and he asks " . . . is it

Paradise/To look on mortal things with an immortal's eyes?" But he finds it impossible to sustain this mood: "Exiled from light, forlorn, I walk in Dublin Town." Yet he knows that, if he had the power to lift the veil, he might find "the fiery rushing chariots of the Lord."

"Michael" is a narrative poem about a boy who leaves Donegal to go to Dublin where he dies in the Easter Rising of 1916. Before going to Dublin, he has a mystical vision as he walks along the seashore:

> The palaces of light were there
> With towers that faded up in air,
> With amethyst and silver spires,
> And casements lit with precious fires,
> And mythic forms with wings outspread
> And faces from which light was shed
> High upon gleaming pillars set
> On turret and on parapet.
> The bells were chiming all around
> And the sweet air was drunk with sound. (361 - 62)

Later in Dublin, the boy finds that his work takes all the joy out of his life, and he longs to return to Donegal. But he remains in Dublin; he meets someone who causes him to become interested in Gaelic legend; as a result, he becomes interested in Irish nationalism; he becomes involved in the Easter Rising of 1916 in which he is killed. The idea that emerges from these rather loosely related events of the story is that, when men die for a cause, a spiritual force takes hold of them and makes them forget themselves and their own selfish goals: "We choose this cause or that, but still/The Everlasting works Its will" (368). Although this poem is only incidentally about the city, the implication is that Michael would have been happier had he never left Donegal. On the other hand, had he not come to Dublin, he would not have sacrificed his life for a noble cause.

When AE visited New York in the 1920's, he was impelled to write a quite different poem about the city; and St. John Ervine may have been right in thinking that a journey would be good for AE. The poem, entitled "New York," shows a new, tighter style, and it also reveals AE's admiration of the architectural wonders of that city. Although the question at the end of the poem is difficult to understand, his poetry has a unity and a firmness of style that places it among AE's best verses:

> With these heaven-assailing spires
> All that was in clay or stone
> Fabled of rich Babylon
> By these children is outdone.
>
> Earth has spilt her fire in these
> To make them of her mightier kind;
> Has she that precious fire to give,
> The starry-pointing Magian mind,
>
> That soared from the Chaldean plains
> Through zones of mystic air, and found
> The Master of the Zodiac,
> The Will that makes the Wheel go round? (414)

The key to the long and enigmatic question which ends the poem and which makes it interesting is the word "Chaldean," for the Chaldeans were noted for their interest in astronomy, astrology, and magic. The skyscrapers of New York are to AE a new form of magic; he asks if the men who built these towers have found some new kind of magic, one similar to that of the ancient Chaldeans. The Master of the Zodiac is probably God, and the "Will that makes the Wheel go round" is His power. An interesting implication of this poem is that all power comes from God and that all men as the children of God, even the architects who built these tall buildings, must find their power in Him.

"In A Strange City" (418 - 19) describes an experience in a city, probably in the United States, which reminds AE of a beloved face, probably his wife's. Both the beauty of the beloved face and that of the city at night come from the same source, but there is also in the poem the suggestion of other experiences in ages past when he speaks of "the honied life it [the heart] had known in ages buried behind," an allusion to his experience in previous lives. The strangeness of this poem makes it one of AE's more interesting achievements. The description of the city at night is vivid and exotic:

> Below the monstrous pagodas builded of
>   blackness and light,
> Whose topmost fires danced with the shining
>   Oreads of night,
> The traffic raced like beast after maddened
>   and blazing beast,

> And a face that had fluttered there afar from
>   the fabulous East,
> Beside me glimmered, lovely, kind, familiar
> —you.

Sometimes, as in "The Cities" (417), he sees hope for a renewal of life in the metropolis:

> Cleansed of their scarlet,
> Absolved of their sin,
> They shall be like crystal
> All stainless within.
>
> Paris and Babel,
> London and Tyre,
> Reborn from the darkness,
> Shall sparkle like fire.

He does not specify the method by which this transformation will occur, and he expresses more of a hope than a prediction.

Two poems deal with the subject of pain and sorrow as aspects of the human condition, and AE was familiar with both. In the short poem "Pain" (82), he writes that he has made a god of pain, just as others have made gods of love, the sun, the giver of rain, and the spirits of hill and grove. Although anguish exists in the touch of this god, "Yet his soul within is sweet." In "The Man to the Angel (84 - 85), the persona of the poem is speaking to an angel, and is contrasting the human with the angelic condition. The angel comes from the pure world, but the impure human condition is better because we learn from pain and sorrow. Not all pain comes from sin; sometimes it comes from aspiring to be great, and we are nearer to the fountain of life because of this pain:

> Pure one, from your pride refrain:
> Dark and lost amid the strife
> I am myriad years of pain
> Nearer to the fount of life. (84)

Turning from pain to love, AE wrote a group of poems concerned with both the physical and the spiritual aspects of this perennial subject. In *Collected Poems*, the earliest poem concerned with this subject is "The Symbol Seduces" (27) in which AE refers to physical love as being seductive and misleading. The "her" of the

poem is physical love, a "symbol of the world's desire," which binds
the soul of fire to the earth. But, when "the robe of Beauty" falls
away and reveals the universal, the spirit, he deserts physical love
for Truth and spiritual love. A sequence of love poems which seem
to be addressed to a single person are: "Warning" (93), "Dream
Love" (94), "Refuge" (95), "The Burning-Glass" (96), "Babylon"
(97), "The Faces of Memory" (99), "The Message" (100), and "Affinity" (103 - 04). In much the same vein all these poems say that
love will triumph because it is eternal and based on spiritual values.
The only one that is at all unusual is "The Burning-Glass" because
AE refers in this poem to the pull of sexual love, "the burning-glass
of womanhod." Though he refuses to yield completely to the temp-
tation of sex, he must "endure the torturing ray." If he can resist
long enough such physical attraction, he will be able to bring his
spirit to hers, "behind the glass, within the glow."

Another group of love poems, not much more interesting than the
first group in terms of ideas or techniques, is "The Vision of Love"
(168), "The Christ-Sword" (169), "Blindness" (170), "Whom We
Worship" (171), "Reflections" (172), "The Morning Star" (173 -
74), "Illusion" (175), "The Dream" (176), and "Mistrust" (177).
AE is not at his best in his love poems: they are somewhat
hackneyed and old-fashioned, reminiscent of the style, idea, and
technique found in Rossetti's love poems. We find in both poets the
same theme about a spiritual love that triumphs over physical love,
but AE is more sincere about this change; and we also note in each
of these poets the same vagueness and misty quality in the diction
and imagery. It may be true that spiritual love is superior to
physical love, but there is a limit to the number of ways it can be
said, and AE has reached that limit.

III   New Themes and Style

A turning point in AE's poetry seems to be promised in a poem
entitled "A New Theme" (198 - 199). Though the style and diction
of the poem do not agree with its thought, AE suggests that his
future poems will be different:

> I fain would leave the tender songs
>   I sang to you of old,
> Thinking the oft-sung beauty wrongs
>   The magic never told.

> And touch no more the thoughts, the moods,
>   That win the easy praise;
> But venture in the untrodden woods
>   To carve the future ways.

We certainly cannot expect much in the way of change from a poem that begins with "I fain would . . . ". The antique diction (*fain, oft-sung, untrodden*) does not indicate that a change in style is coming very fast or very soon. But a change did come with the volume entitled *Gods of War*, a group of poems inspired by World War I. Those included in *Collected Poems* are the following: "Gods of War" (236 - 38), "Ares" (241 - 43), "Statesmen" (254 - 55), "Shadows and Lights" (247 - 50), "Battle Ardour" (239), "Chivalry" (246), "Tragedy" (253), "Forboding" (244 - 45), and "Apocalyptic, 1915" (251 - 52). The first poem in the volume, "Gods of War," compares World War I with the war between Carthage and Rome. Modern warships, airplanes, and submarines now add to the conflict; but, though the weapons are modern, the war is still the old battle between good and evil which no one wins but the Devil. Christ is defied again, and the gods of war are now fashionable.

This new subject seems to have brought about a development in AE's poetic style which was promised but not delivered in "A New Theme." Although he does not get completely away from the older style and although he still speaks of the ancestral self quite often, his style becomes firmer. This development is seen in "Battle Ardour," a companion piece to Yeats's "An Irish Airman Foresees His Death," in which AE describes the ecstasy of an airman as he fights and dies in an aerial battle. He is free of the earth and finds triumph even in depth; he is fighting not for the "right of kings" but for the experience itself:

> Not now it battles for the rights of kings.
> This ecstasy is all its own; to be
> Quit of itself, mounted upon the power
> That, like Leviathan, breaks from the deep
> Primeval and all conquering. He dies!
> Yet has he conquered in that very hour.
> He and his foeman the same tryst do keep.
> His foemen are his brothers in the skies. (239)

The syntax is more modern (with the exception of "tryst do keep");
the vocabulary is no longer antique (except for *tryst*); and the run-
on lines help to break up the usual regular rhythms of the poem.
AE's poem lacks the originality and the singing quality of Yeats's
poem, but for AE it is an achievement.

AE's purpose is still didactic in these poems, and his ideas about
the futility and the chicanery of war emerge in them. "Statesmen"
is an attack on the men in power who tell us they oppose war but
who become in their pride as base as the foe they fight. As he says
so often, we become like that which we contemplate, or, as he says
in "Tragedy," "None ever hated in the world but came/To every
baseness of the foe he fought" (253). Pride is the cause of war; the
only antidote is love and humility:

> The pride that builded Babylon of Egypt was
>   the mighty child:
> The beauty of the Attic soul in many a lovely
>   city smiled.
> The empire that is built in pride shall call
>   imperial pride to birth,
> And with that shadow of itself must fight for
>   empire of the earth.
> Fight where ye will on earth or sea, beneath
>   the wave, above the hills,
> The foe ye meet is still yourselves, the blade
>   ye forged the sword that kills. (255)

In "Shadows and Lights," AE asks if the divine powers are responsible for the war; he concludes that they are not; for we humans
cause the strife when our vision fails and when we cannot see the
divine purpose in the world. In "Chivalry," he compares the
chivalric way of conducting war in the past with the modern war-
fare of the Iron Age, and he seems to think that the wars of the past
were not so grim as those of the present.

"Apocalyptic, 1915" is probably the most difficult of these poems
and one of the most interesting. Based on the sixth chapter of
Revelations, which describes the four horsemen of the Apocalypse
whose horses are white, bright red, black, and the last a pale horse
whose rider is Death, the idea of the poem is vague—couched in
symbolic language. But AE seems to be saying that the result of the
war will be a new society rising from the ruins of the old corrupt

one. Men in war may laugh only if they are courageous in the presence of pain and death and have the will to be reborn as immortals.

> If the black horse's rider reign,
> Or the pale horse's rider fire
> His burning arrows, with disdain
> Laugh. You have come to your desire,
> To the last test which yields the right
> To walk amid the halls of light.
>
> You, who have made of earth your star,
> Cry out, indeed, for hopes made vain:
> For only those can laugh who are
> The strong Initiates of Pain,
> Who know that mighty god to be
> Sculptor of immortality. (252)

Though the meaning of this poem is far from clear in logical terms, the compression and the sharpness of the images reveals a distinctly modern technique.

Another class of AE's poems was inspired by the Irish Rebellion and by the Civil War which followed it. There are not too many of these poems, possibly because AE was too busy during these years working for a solution to the Home Rule problem. The most important of these poems is "Salutation," a poem about the 1916 Easter Rising; which will be discussed in Chapter 6 in connection with AE's work and writings that relate to this eventful struggle. In a poem called "Waste" (352), he describes the waste of human life and energy in what we guess to be the Civil War of 1922:

> Had they but died for some
> High image in the mind,
> Not spilt the sacrifice
> For words hollow as wind! (352)

Though AE was a nationalist and though he felt that Irish myth and legend were important heritages of Ireland, he opposed revolution, bloodshed, and violence even in the cause of Irish independence. That he felt the future was more important than the past is made clear in a poem entitled "On Behalf of Some Irishmen Not Followers of Tradition":

> We would no Irish sign efface,
> But yet our lips would gladlier hail
> The firstborn of the Coming Race
> Than the last splendour of the Gael.
> No blazoned banner we unfold—
> One charge alone we give to youth,
> Against the sceptered myth to hold
> The golden heresy of truth. (230)

As if to balance this poem, AE places immediately after it the poem "An Irish Face" in which he reflects about the sorrow in the face of a woman he has met. Such sorrow is not only from the unhappiness in her own life but from the sorrows of the race—those of Deirdre, Cuchulain, and the Wild Geese.[21] Contemplation of this face makes us realize the strength of our tradition, but how can these two seemingly opposing positions on tradition be reconciled? AE realizes the strength and power of tradition, but he also insists that tradition is of value only if it leads to a greater country and to a better race.

A number of AE's poems do not fit into any of the usual patterns, and one of the most interesting of these is "The Dark Lady" which appeared in *The House of the Titans and Other Poems.*[22] The point of departure is Shakespeare's Sonnet 134, in which we read about someone, presumably a woman, who has enslaved both the poet and his friend, presumably a man. With this sonnet as a start, AE's story unfolds in his narrative poem in which a woman of the court of Queen Elizabeth tells of her love for Shakespeare. After a learned gentleman of the court has introduced her to "the latest prince of speech," she finds him more interesting than the court; and she falls in love with his mind and his spirit. She avoids physical love with him because she fears that it will affect their relationship and that she will lose his spiritual love:

> And though I was all love I shrank from that,
> The mating of lips and body, lest having all
> I should have less than love; in the king's bed
> Be absent from his court. (48)

But, while she reveled in the wealth of his creative mind, a young man came to court who captured Shakespeare's heart, and a kind of homosexual attachment is suggested:

And I grew sick
Seeing the dawn of an unnatural love,
The kind that marred the Grecian genius, and closed
The nobleness of mind that had begun
With Homer's tale. (50)

In a vain attempt to regain her lost love, she offers herself physically to Shakespeare but finds no joy in the act. Since her attempt is unsuccessful, she turns her attention to the young man, her rival, and seduces him in an attempt to take him away from her beloved:

I yielded to him, became
A mistress unto two, one godlike in mind
And one, the outer image of a god. (52)

When Shakespeare finally discovers her affair, he is terribly hurt:

And then at last one day I met the other
And he had known, and never was there face
So ravaged, and my heart in every beat
Let rain a drop all fiery red. (53)

Never, she says, "Was I so lost from myself, so terribly his." After Shakespeare calls her a whore ("He threw at me a single word."), he leaves her, never to return; but she feels that she has won a victory, "Slaying the unnatural with the natural love." She concludes with a reference to the scene in Dante's *Divine Comedy*, in which Paolo and Francesca, the unlawful lovers, are blown about by violent winds as punishment for their sins on earth. She says that she would be content to have that fate if Shakespeare could be her partner in that final torment. She has a dream in which she is thus blown about; however, her partner is not Shakespeare, but her rival for Shakespeare's love. When she awakens, her pillow is wet with her tears.

This poem, so unusual for AE, is so very fine that we wonder what would have happened had he been carried away more often from his accustomed themes. The constant reiteration of the old theme of the fall of man and of his ability to return to the divine, if only he would, weakens the force of AE's total poetic output. But, from time to time, his lines leap from the page, seize the imagination, and fall upon the ear with compelling accents. "The Dark

Lady" shows clearly that he had the ability to write other than in a
mystical vein and that he is at his best when he is least didactic—when he depends upon the worth of his poetic ideas to convey
the true sense of his wisdom. It is unfortunate that he did not more
often listen to his own words when he said

> And only the teaching
> That never was spoken
> Is worthy thy reaching,
> The fountain unbroken.[23]

CHAPTER 4

AE's Drama and Fiction

T HE imaginative works of AE, other than his poetry, are
    included mainly in four volumes. *Deirdre* (1903) is a play
based on the Irish legend about Deirdre and Naisi; *The Mask of
Apollo* (1905), a collection of tales; and two books which might
loosely be called novels are *The Interpreters* (1922) and *The Avatars*
(1933). The last two are not exactly works of imaginative literature,
but they do develop AE's mystic philosophy.

I Deirdre: *The Drama*

Deirdre[1] is taken from the Irish legend of the Red Branch, a part
of the Ulster Cycle; the name of the story is *Longes Mac Nusnig* or
The Exile of the Sons of Usnech.[2] The play follows the story closely;
and AE adds little that is new. The story concerns Deirdre, who, according to prophecy, is fated to cause the destruction of the Red
Branch. King Conchobar cannot bear to have her killed, as she is
very beautiful; and he therefore has her hidden. She meets Naisi,
they fall in love at first sight, and Naisi refuses to believe the
prophecy. When the King hears of their love, he becomes angry and
vows revenge. Meanwhile, Deirdre and Naisi have fled across the
sea to Alba (Scotland) where they live for three years. When they
are informed by Fergus (the stepfather of Conchobar) that King
Conchobar has forgiven them, they return to Ireland against Deirdre's wishes because she distrusts Conchobar and fears that Naisi is
returning to certain death. Although Conchobar had truly forgiven
them because he had heard that Deirdre's beauty had faded, when
he sees that she is as beautiful as she was before her departure, his
anger returns, and he causes Naisi and his brothers to be put to
death. Deirdre dies of grief, and Fergus returns to kill Conchobar
for his treachery. Lavarcam, Deirdre's foster mother, says that Deirdre will be remembered for her sorrow, Conchobar for his
treachery.

AE's career as a dramatist was based on this single play. The plot is slight and simple, depending purely on suffering for its tragic effect. The movement is slow, and it follows the theory of Yeats that drama should not be an excitement of the nerves but the establishment of a mood. The characters are not particularly moving, having been changed little from the legend. Though the work is in prose, the language is poetic in places. For example, at the beginning of Act I, Lavercam says: "The harp has but three notes; and after sleep and laughter, the last sound is of weeping." This statement sets the mood of the play, which moves relentlessly to the end, where Deirdre's fears are confirmed as all of the principal persons die. There is a sense of foreboding in the play, which is typical of much of Irish tragedy, including even the modern playwrights such as Synge and O'Casey. The chief interest in this play is its Irish legendary subject matter, for Yeats and Russell agreed as to the purpose of Irish drama at this time in the early days of the Abbey Theatre: Their aim was to awaken the heroic sense of the Irish people by acquainting them dramatically with their ancient heritage.

II The Mask of Apollo: *Short Stories*

The Mask of Apollo,[3] contains stories which had been previously printed in various journals; the prefatory note states that this collection represents AE's first attempts at writing fiction. He had hoped that he could improve the stories; but characteristically, felt that the mystical mood in which they were written had passed, and they were merely reprinted. They come from a variety of sources, including Greek, Indian, Irish, and Jewish ones. The first story, "The Mask of Apollo," purports to be from Greek legend; it tells of Apollo's coming to earth, his taking the form of a village priest, and his answering the questions of those who come to see him; and it represents, therefore, AE's characteristic theme of the avatar and prefigures the work of that name.

When Agathon, working in the fields, asks Apollo why he worships Zeus, Apollo replies that Zeus does not live in the air alone but in all of Nature, in every flower and blade of grass. He also explains the nature of poetry to Damon, the shepherd, and the nature of love to two lovers, Dion and Neaera. To Damon, Apollo explains that the poet is privileged to hear the music of the gods and that he must teach their songs to his people. This idea is, of course, based on the Romantic theory of the nature of the poet that is expressed in

Wordsworth's "Preface to Lyrical Ballads" which also depicts the poet as the mediator between man and the divine. To the lovers, Apollo says that each of the gods gave something to man at his creation and that Aphrodite contributed the soul which makes men and women attractive to one another. As this recital indicates, the story is a parable of man's spiritual origin and of his spiritual destiny.

In "The Cave of Lilith," a story of attempted seduction, we have a parable about the evil possibilities in man when he falls from the divine. Lilith, the temptress, is wise in the ways of sin and pleasure; but she attempts to seduce the Wise One without success. She boasts that "[her] . . . illusions are sweeter to them [those who yield to her temptation] than truth. I offer every soul its own shadow. . . . I am made up of hopes and fears. The subtle princes lay out their plans of conquest in my cave, and there the hero dreams, and there the lovers of all time write in flame their history. I am wise, holding all experience, to tempt, to blind, to terrify" (10).

Lilith is a mythological figure who comes to us out of Rabbinical literature and the Kabbalah.[4] According to one tradition, she was the first wife of Adam and was replaced by Eve; according to another, she was the bride of Samael, but adultery between Samael and Eve, Adam and Lilith, is suggested. She is obviously symbolic of the sexual appetite and of the animal nature of man and woman. From this ancient story, AE extracts the following wisdom: "From the Wise One I learned that the truest wisdom is to wait, to work, and to will in secret. Those who are voiceless today, tomorrow shall be eloquent, and the earth shall hear them. Of these three truths, the hardest to learn is the silent will. Let us seek for the highest truth" (13).

In "The Story of a Star," the narrator, Robert, is in a little cathedral town where he has come to get away from the noise of the city. In this peaceful setting he thinks of the Indian philosophy of Maya or illusion, and he is permitted to see in his vision the childhood of the world. As he pierces the veil of nature, he sees the birth of a planet:

At first silence, and then an inner music, and then the sounds of song through the vastness of its orbit grew as many in number as there were stars at gaze. Avenues and vistas of sound! They reeled to and fro. They poured from a universal stillness quick with unheard things. They rushed forth and broke into a myriad voices gay with childhood. From age and the eternal

they rushed forth into youth. They filled the void with revelling and exultation. In rebellion they then returned and entered the dreadful Fountain.
Again they came forth, and the sounds faded into whispers; they rejoiced
once again, and died into silence. (17 - 21)

During a visit to this spiritual planet Robert asks himself about the
meaning and end of life; and he is informed by one of the race
which lives on the new planet that the aim of life is creation from
whence comes our joy. Ultimately, he is told, the earth on which we
live will be transmuted into a spiritual world like this planet. Thus
this story once again presents the vision of what life on earth can be,
a divine breath in the infinite life of God.

"A Dream of Angus Oge," a simple story taken from Irish legend,
is about a boy who has a vision of life among the immortals (25 -
30). The next two stories, "The Mediation of Ananda" (33 - 37)
and "The Midnight Blossom" (41 - 45), are Indian; and the first
one is about Ananda, the ascetic, who is inspired by a priest to per-
form an act of meditation which causes four acts of love: a great
king forgives an enemy he is about to execute, a child restores hope
to a prisoner by a gift of flowers, two lovers bring hope to an old
woman who was once beautiful by speaking in her presence and
reminding her of her own youth, and a teacher speaks to his disciples in the presence of a leper and makes him happy. In the second Indian story, four persons accompany a yogi up a mountain
where they see a midnight blossom, a holy flower, which is the symbol of universal harmony and the lost innocence of the world. The
last story, "The Childhood of Apollo," takes us back to Greece (49 -
53), and it simply relates how Apollo became a god and how
Diotima, the sybil, reveals to him the Ancient Beauty in the form of
a light from heaven.

III   The Interpreters

All of these early stories are short and simple, and all of them
reinforce AE's mystical philosophy. *The Interpreters* (1922) is a
futurist symposium, rather complicated, which investigates the
relationship between "the politics of time" and "the politics of eternity." AE said that it was written during the war "when everybody
was talking about God and their nation and I tried to speculate how
the Oversoul might affect the nationalities in politics."[5] He does not
say which war, but the context of the story suggests the Irish
Rebellion of 1921, although AE says in the preface that *The Inter-*

preters was set in a future century in order for him to achieve a disinterested and impartial approach in his narrative.

As the story opens, a young poet named Lavelle is hurrying through the streets of a European city; and his mission is connected with the revolt of a small country against the tyranny of an empire which had long held it in subjection. The allusion to Great Britain and Ireland is clear, but AE never mentions these names. When the revolt fails, Lavelle finds himself in prison with some of his fellow revolutionists. As the night wears on, they discuss the rebellion and present various interpretations of the event, which accounts for the name of the story.

The result is a symposium about the central question of the book: What is the relationship between the events of the day ("the politics of time") and the divine mind which rules the world ("the politics of eternity")? The basic assumption of the book is that there *is* such a divine mind which does rule the world and that everything that happens in the world, including wars and rebellions, are related to it. This view is summarized in the first epigraph on the title page in a line from St. Paul: "In Him we live and move and have our being." The second epigraph is the question posed by the anarchist, Leroy: "What relation have the politics of time to the politics of eternity?" The third epigraph points to the basic ethical concern of the book, a question asked by Lavelle: "How can right find its appropriate might?"

The speakers in the symposium are characterized more by their ideas than by their physical appearance, emotions, or actions, yet they have individuality and verisimilitude. AE admitted in the preface that he was more interested in ideas than in character or plot. Representing various points of view, the speakers are, according to AE, the various members of a divided personality, or "the scattered portions of the one nature dramatically sundered as the soul is in dream."[6] The more important speakers are Lavelle, who seems to represent the poetic side of AE's personality; Rian, an architect, who may represent the artistic aspect of AE's nature; Leroy, an Anarchist; Culain, a Socialist who looks like James Connolly, labor leader and hero of the Easter Rising of 1916; and Brehon, an historian who seems to represent the great Irish historian, Standish O'Grady. One other person enters the conversation, an imperialist named Heyt, who has been captured and imprisoned by mistake and who is released at the end of the book. He has obviously been included to represent the imperialist point of view and to provide conflict between his conservative ideas and the

ideas of the others who are more radical and more inclined toward
the nationalist point of view.[7]

The setting is a prison cell where a number of prisoners are herd-
ed together in various attitudes: some sleeping, some listening to
the discussion which continues through the night. As the battle outside continues, the symposium begins with a dialogue between
Lavelle and Leroy, who are opposites in their thinking. Lavelle, a
poet, is a romantic and an idealist, who finds in everything a divine
unity which is basically good. Leroy is an Anarchist, a diabolist, and
"an idealist without faith in society" who believes in God; and he
holds that the various points of view expressed by those in the discussion are various manifestations of the relationships of the
speakers to God. An Anarchist who believes that society suppresses
the individual, he represents AE's fear of the state.

Lavelle believes that the revolution has been the result of divine
inspiration. Revolutions do not occur as the result of our
relationships with people we know personally but as the result of
ideas and influences which come to us from the minds and spirits of
many people, the group mind. The powers which rule us from
above function more through the group than through the individual. When nations arise and give a feeling of unity to many
people, the result is a national character developed through a group
identity. The legends and myths of a nation are the embodiment of
national inspiration which manifests itself today in the imaginations
of the poet and the visions of the mystic.

Rian, the architect, agrees with Lavelle in two respects. First, for
both of them imagination precedes creation. Just as the idea is the
parent of action for Lavelle, for Rian the building or the city which
he creates on earth must first be found in his imagination. Second,
Rian agrees that the individual is powerless by himself: "Architects
by themselves do not build cities" (57). Likewise, statesmen create
civilizations by unifying the people into a harmonious effort.

When Brehon, the historian, asks if the will to enforce a national
ideal is inspired by divine powers, Lavelle replies that this inspiration is often the only way an idea can become a reality on earth. In
the present struggle, an alien and materialistic culture is trying to
force its mechanistic way of life on a small country which has a
spiritual and heroic culture; and for this reason Lavelle participated
in the revolt. Undoubtedly AE was thinking of Great Britain and
Ireland in his rather simplistic identification of the great power with
mechanism and the small power with spirit and heroism.

Heyt, the imperialist, rejects these ideas as Romantic imaginations, for, since nature and the "world soul" have decreed the
world state, it is useless to struggle against it.

". . . You cry out against the world state which Nature has made like the
lion, but the will of the world soul is seen in the organisms it endows with
power. The might of an organism is a measure of its rightness, for no
organism could grow to power through centuries maintaining itself against
the evolutionary purpose. The upholding of a regional ideal is like the dis-
play of a ruined house inhabited by a few shadowy ghosts. If Nature was
with your thought it would have bestowed power on it, but the world soul
has decreed the world state." (65 - 66)

This doctrine is, of course, the old one that might makes right and
that whatever is according to Nature prevails and should prevail.
Heyt, the imperialist, obviously expresses the opposite of what AE
believes; and the author reveals some sophistication which his early
work lacked—the ability to put what he does not believe into the
words of the antagonist. Against the protests of the others, Heyt
maintains that the world state is the inevitable result of evolutionary
processes and is justified by the design of nature. Just as an orator
can unify an audience temporarily, the state can bring about a permanent unity in the beings which compose it. This unity is a
product of the Divine Mind which wills the unity of all the people
in the state. The world state is the vehicle through which the cosmic
mind shapes history, operating through its ability to control many
people.

Leroy opposes this idea with the concept that the individual will
is the ultimate value in the universe; the world state would destroy
this individualism, thus dehumanizing man. Lavelle also opposes
the world state and believes it will fail, but on other grounds. Since
the national will derives its power from tradition, it will successfully
oppose the world state. To Lavelle, national tradition is very important; for a nation to lose its tradition would be like a man losing his
soul.

Heyt is not awed by the beauty of legend and myth for they
belong to the past and are no more valuable than the discoveries
science will make in the future. The conflict here is between
history, legend, and nationalism on one side and on the other,
science, the future, and internationalism. In a real sense, the
struggle of ideas between Lavelle and Heyt is a projection of the

struggle within AE at this time; but it also is a microcosmic projection of the struggle that all humanity faces today.

A new voice is heard as Culain, the Socialist, says that the ultimate value is to be found in humanity itself. The power of empire
does not descend from above but comes from below out of the
depths of humanity, from the common people who suffer to provide
this great power. The destiny of humanity is self-realization through
beneficent institutions which grow out of human pity for human
suffering. This self-realization will not come from the divine mind
above as Heyt believes, nor out of the legends of the past as Lavelle
believes, nor out of the individual soul as Leroy believes: It will
come only through social action. In the perfect society which Culain
envisions, man would once again be pure and beautiful, "a mightier
Adam or Heavenly Man." Pity and compassion are the human vir-
tues closest to the yearning of the limited soul for its lost unity with
the oversoul; pity and compassion will give rise to the new social
order; and this new order will, in turn, make possible the reunification of the human soul with the ancestral soul. Leroy objects to this
view by saying that he is "skeptical about all methods of achieving
spiritual ends by material means" (96). Culain replies that, if Com-
munism comes with collective property, it will be the result of a
new spiritual attitude in which selfishness is replaced by altruism:
"The spiritual change comes and must come before the material
change" (97). We are evolving to this spiritual state; when we reach
it, the purity of earth will reflect it; and no one will then be selfish.
When another prisoner named Rudd expresses the feelings of the
common man who has been reared in an orthodox religion by saying that the priests will tell him about God and the next world,
Leroy replies that the God to which he refers has been dead for
many years; thus he disposes of conventional religion as far as AE is
concerned.

The symposium is interrupted by the noise of the destruction of
an airplane by a rebel plane, which is in turn destroyed. From time
to time, AE inserts bits of similar action to provide a contrast with
the quiet battle of wits going on inside the cell. Leroy calls the attack by the rebel plane heroic, and he wishes that he could leave
this life in such a blaze of glory. From violent action such as this
stems self-knowledge and self-realization; it is in this manner that
the individual can best learn to know himself. Leroy rejects any
value that does not arise in the individual consciousness, and he
refers continually to his "Dark Angel," the spirit of revolt which is
characteristic of the man that is most individualistic.

When Rian turns to Brehon to ask him if he can reconcile the conflicting ideas which have been presented in the symposium, Brehon replies that they are reconciled in his own being because he has held all of these ideas himself at one time or another. But he cannot reconcile them in words now, for no single mental process can mirror the truth in speech: " 'Speech is not like a mirror which reflects fully the form before it; but in speech things, which by their nature are innumerable and endless, are indicated by brief symbols' " (122). But Brehon does attempt a reconciliation in terms of a distinction between three qualities of the human world and life: matter, energy, and spirit. Behind these three qualities, we can see only Deity; the three are as mysterious as Deity; and they are manifested in human thought and action. Therefore, each of the disputants speaks in terms of one of these qualities: " 'All that is substance in us aspires to the ancestral beauty. All that is power in us desires to become invincible. All that is consciousness longs for fullness of being' " (123). The first quality, matter, corresponds to the position of Lavelle and Culain; the second, energy, to Heyt, and the third, spirit, to Leroy. Brehon concludes that this trinity when exalted and unified leads to the concept of Deity. Men who aspire to this unity are self-sufficient, and the purpose of Nature is to produce such great men. He seems to lean to the side of Lavelle and Leroy when he says that this apparent purpose in Nature seems to justify the freedom of the individual and the self-government of nations.

Brehon, who appears to be the moderator for the discussion, summarizes AE's position. When Lavelle says that men must fight for what they believe to be right or their ideals will perish, Brehon advocates passive resistance; for men can be "fighters in the spirit and use immortal powers" (135). Men lose their spiritual qualities when they take part in physical violence and become like their adversaries, but those who are gentle have greater influence than those who are violent: " 'The avatars of the spirit, the Christs and Buddhas, do more by single gentleness than conquerors with armies do, and build more enduring kingdoms in the spirit of man' " (140). When Lavelle objects that distinctions of nationality are obscured by the Transcendental ideal of Brehon, the old historian replies that mankind is evolving toward the fulfillment of its spiritual greatness; therefore, nothing really related to its essential humanity will be lost. The divine law of the universe will regulate all diverse cultures; and, when these cultures are rightly related to one another, they will all coexist in harmony. Once men are governed

by their ancestral selves they will no longer be concerned with the
politics of time, for they will be governed purely by the politics of
eternity. But men must continually infuse politics with the "expanding spiritual consciousness," so that the spiritual energies will
not be perverted. If any group or race is excluded, these energies
will be perverted and will poison the source of life.

Brehon believes that there are powers in nature which will serve
us if we live in accordance with the laws of nature, but these same
powers will turn on us if we offend them and will bring about
cataclysmic events such as earthquakes. But for those who turn to
the spirit, there is no loss of strength: " 'In the ascent to Heaven, as
Socrates said, we create a multitude of high and noble thoughts, our
own nature expanding until at last we attain a science which is
equal to a beauty so vast' " (150). But until we reach the heights of
the spirit our view is distorted. " 'Those who would mould life in
accord with divine nature must remember until their faculties are
perfected they look at it through the stained glass of the personal,
and be watchful lest they limit in imagination that which is
boundless' " (152).

The connection between this book and AE's poetry is the poem,
"Michael," which is supposed to have been written in prison by
Lavelle. These lines summarize the message of *The Interpreters:*

> We choose this cause or that, but still
> The Everlasting works its will.
> The slayer and the slain may be
> Knit in a secret harmony.
> What does the spirit urge us to?
> Some sacrifice that may undo
> The bonds that hold us to the clay,
> And limit life to this cold day?
> Some for a gentle dream will die:
> Some for an empire's majesty:
> Some for a loftier humankind,
> Some to be free as cloud or wind,
> Will leave their valley, climb their slope.
> Whate'er the deed, whate'er the hope,
> Through all the varied battle cries
> A Shepherd with a single voice
> Still draws us nigh the Gates of Gold
> That lead unto the heavenly fold. (171 - 72)[8]

At dawn, the prisoners are informed that they are to die; that the
arsenal in which they are imprisoned is to be destroyed; and that
their captors can take no prisoners with them when they leave.

Heyt's identity is discovered and he is released, but the others are to be joined in death to the force which united them in life.

IV The Avatars: *"futuristic fantasy"*

The Interpreters, which can hardly be truly classified as a novel, is more of a dialogue like those of Plato: It is a fictional account of a group of men in a given situation who develop philosophical ideas about human life as a Transcendental experience on earth. AE was capable of writing fiction, but he was too much interested in ideas to write a novel in the ordinary sense of the genre. *The avatars* (1933) is a little closer to being a novel, but its ideology is still more important than either plot or characters. He called it a "futuristic fantasy," and the center of the story consists of two avatars who visit the earth. An avatar in the Hindu religion is a god who comes to the earth in human form; the word is from Sanskrit, according to Eglinton, and it means literally "he who goes down or passes beyond."[9] This word AE uses often, and it derived from his interest in Theosophy.

The avatars in the narrative are never seen very clearly, but their presence is felt distinctly. The epigraph, taken from Claude Monet, the French Impressionist painter, reads, "The Light is the real person in the picture." This quotation suggests that the avatars are like the light in an Impressionist painting: spiritual and luminous, it is not fully realized nor made definite. AE's prefatory note makes this interpretation clear: "No more than an artist could paint the sun at noon could I imagine so great beings. But as a painter may suggest the light on hill or wood, so in this fantasy I tried to imagine the spiritual excitement created by two people who pass dimly through the narrative, spoken of by others but not speaking themselves."[10]

As the narrative begins, Paul Heron, an artist, is heading for the West of Ireland in an automobile and is leaving behind him the dark and dismal city. He was once one of the slaves in the factories of the city, but he has escaped to become an artist, and Michael Conaire, who has been like an older brother to him, has helped him do so. As Paul Heron travels through the winter landscape, he sees two heavenly beings in a vision. They are the avatars, "crested with many-coloured lights, gigantic forms that seemed shaped from some banished and exquisite fire. They held swords of wavering flame as if guardians of some precious thing" (4).

Paul describes his vision to Michael, who explains to him its meaning. These beings, he says, are *avatars* who have come to reveal the spiritual nature of the Irish race to itself. They are not merely gods; they are pivotal figures who are destined to change the course of a nation's history. Helen of Troy, Alexander, Cuchulain—all were avatars by this definition, according to AE. From the conversation between Paul and Michael, we comprehend that they represent two aspects of AE's own nature. Paul, who represents the young AE as an artist, is fleeing from the mechanical and industrial world which enslaves men; his destination is the mystical quiet of the Western, Irish country; and he reflects AE's annual flights from Dublin into the loveliness of Donegal. Michael, representing the older AE, is the seer who has penetrated the secrets of the mystical world. Both men are visionaries; and they also agree in their basic attitude which is Romantic, anti-industrial, and spiritual.

The story which unfolds concerns the development of a new religion in the West of Ireland, one that originates in the actions of the two avatars. One of the avatars, Aodh, who comes to view Paul's painting, is a changeling, about fourteen years old, with unusual spiritual powers. Also a visionary, he refuses to attend school because he does not wish to be confined in a room and separated from the influence of nature. The other avatar, the girl Aoife, is a friend of Michael Conaire's daughter Olive. We do not learn much about her except that Olive compares her to Helen of Troy because "she sets fire to all about her" (97). These two avatars are at the center of the story, and the action consists of the conversations of the other characters about their activities.

The other characters include the following: Felim Carew is a poet who is accepted into the mystical fraternity when he identifies three of Paul's paintings. The first is the cottage he saw on his way to the West "aureoled with light with its divine guardians holding their swords of wavering flame." The second is of a mountain crested with fire, which Paul and Aodh had seen. The third was a portrait of Aodh. Michael explains that these paintings represent mystical visions into Ildathatch, the Many-Colored Land, the lost Eden of the world when men were divine. The earth was then a living being with a soul and a spirit, and gods and fairies were numerous. But men have now drifted from that blessed state, and only poets and painters can see into the ancient spirit world. Carew identifies the three paintings: " 'A divine child! A manger, heavenly guarded! A holy mountain' " (53).

Carew introduces Paul to another artist named Mark and to his wife Mary. Mark is a mystical sculptor who uses a different medium but whose attitude is similar to Paul's. One of Mark's figures is described in the following passage. "An uncouth animal shape was heaving its haunches out of clay with its forefeet straining against the earth for complete emancipation. And itself seemed to be changing; for as in the centaur the human rises out of the animal, so from the monstrous earth-born creature rose a lovely winged figure with face cast upward as if it was beating its way into air. As the monster had struggled out of earth and rock so out of the brute the psyche was winging its way into the heavenly aether" (77). The introduction of Mark and Mary seems to serve no other purpose than to provide this symbol of man's upward climb from the animal to the spiritual condition.

When the philosopher Michael Gregor is brought into the story he provides contrast and conflict. He is a skeptic, but he would like to believe the Transcendental doctrine of his friends. He believes with Schopenhauer that the will is the fundamental reality in human nature and that it is unlike our imaginations, which are unreal and transient. Though he has been in a position of power and responsibility, he has surrendered his worldly power and pleasure through the exercise of the will. Gregor would like to believe the dreams of his friends, but he is afraid that his dreams will betray him and that he will fall back into his former worldly existence. It is only the will which he trusts to keep himself pure. A Stoic among Transcendentalists, he provides a dialectical pole for the discussion of the good life which is central to the book.

The conflict which arises involves the characters of the novel who have been introduced and the harsh masters of the state who care nothing for the spirit of man. Aoife and Aodh, both now grown, have departed; but they are to lead the country to a new spiritual revelation. Rumors of the movements of the two divine persons begin to arrive from the far south, and their movements can be traced by these rumors. Wherever they are, they bring with them happiness and loveliness, dance and song; and the people who meet them are transfigured and exalted. Carew attempts to explain to Paul the meaning of the revelation that is at hand, and recites some of his poems which describe the holy experience. They are, of course, AE's own poems. When we meet the gods, says Carew, we will not abase ourselves before them: "What are the gods," he asks, "but elder brothers to us? We are of the same lineage. I will pay reverence to those who transcend me, but I will not abase myself." (125)

When Gregor tells Paul of a plot to bring all of the rebels under the control of the state, they go together to a festival where Aoife and Aodh are appearing; and, in a battle between the forces of the state and the avatars, Paul is knocked unconscious and Gregor killed, "the first martyr for a faith he did not hold" (133). Aodh and Aoife disappear, no one knows where; but a year later we are informed that a new religion has grown up around the legend of Aoife and Aodh and that a temple filled with works of art is to be built where they disappeared. A rich culture has developed about their story that is "so harmonious in its parts that it seems almost the product of one mind" (136); and this "one mind" is the divine mind or *anima mundi*.

Two new characters are introduced into the novel before it ends. The first is the American Clubborn whose money made a new temple possible for the religion founded by the avatars. The second is Rory Lavelle, whose uncle was the poet Lavelle, who had died years before in the revolt described in *The Interpreters*. All of these characters discuss the avatars and their new religion, and Paul describes in particular the influence of Aodh. He compares him to Krishna, who said, "I am born through my own maya, the mystic power of self ideation." Aodh's act of imagination is like the act of creation in the mind of the poet and inspires creativity in others. " 'It was, I believe, to kindle a creative imagination that Aodh was born into our sphere' " (150). Life had been frozen by the monstrous mechanism of the state, and Aodh had arrived to revive the creative energy in man and to free him from his bondage.

The story of Aodh and Aoife has had spiritual results, but Michael Conaire sees that others may distort its meaning and profane it because beauty is always pursued by beasts who pervert the divine to their own evil purposes. Hardly had he said these words when a man enters whom many have recognized as George Moore. He is a famous story-teller and he speaks "in the soft caressing voice of those who are accustomed to speak to women more than to men." (169) His characteristic "Hail and farewell," identify him as Moore. He sees the tale only in its romantic and sexual implications:

"The romance of it! They went rambling together in a country of lakes and hills. Of course she became his mistress. But none here believe it. They get angry at the thought. They will have it the companionship was platonic. But you and I understand life. We know that platonic affection is the most enchanting approach to bodily love. People imagine wonderful things about each other. They seem to be groping for the heavens and suddenly find themselves in each other's arms. Religion, philosophy, poetry, music, all the arts indeed beget lovely phantoms who lead us delicately to a simple act." (170)

Characteristically, AE puts the opposing point of view in the speech of one of his characters. Carew is the spokeman for AE: " 'That thing has worms slinking through its veins, not blood. It would pollute the earth to bury him in it. He ought to be dropped off the planet with demons clawing him all the way to the bottomless pit.' " (171) Thus AE at the same time disposes of the naturalism of Moore and shows us that good has its necessary evil opposite in life. As Conaire says, beauty is always pursued by beasts who pervert the divine to their evil purpose.

This view brings him to a criticism of Christianity which, in the opinion of both Conaire and AE, dwells too much on pain and megative emotions: " 'Pain if it comes naturally to us here, if it is endured with resignation, brings its own nobility. But to seek it for its own sake, that is devilish. The brooding on agonies, martyrdoms and crucifixions leads the soul into sinister by-ways. Out of the brooding on the tortured God was born the mentality which made the dark ages hideous with religious persecutions, with the rack, the stake, and the martyr's fire' " (173). Even great writers like Dante and Milton have degraded the mysteries they seek to represent in such works as *The Divine Comedy* and *Paradise Lost*, respectively, by depicting the negative aspects of the Christian mystery. AE would accept the love of God and Christ, as well as love for his fellow man; but he rejects the view that life is sinful and the concept of man's necessary redemption through grace. Man has grace within him—if only he will know it and use it.

When Paul asks why we are given such mysteries if they are to be degraded in this way, Conaire replies in Blakean terms that it is only by the fusion of opposites that the soul becomes strong: " 'When the soul enters a higher heaven in its own nature it must have insight into lower deeps. We descend into these, not to surrender to them, not to be overcome, but to bring about a harmony or fusion of opposites. I think only by this fusion of opposites does the soul itself become strong. We cannot go from earth leaving behind us untransmuted the elements and forces the soul had gathered about itself, the dross and slime of its life' " (175).

This passage represents the embarrassment of the mystic or of the Transcendentalist by the fact of evil in the world. In a world which is essentially good, how can we explain evil? Like Blake, AE explains it by a polarization of opposites: Without evil, what is good? How can good exist if there be no evil? It is only through the awareness of evil and the determination to transcend it that the

mystic finds the good. Although this statement is what AE means by
"the fusion of opposites," it is not really as much a fusion as a
transcending of evil by good.

Conaire summarizes the meaning of the avatars when he says that
they left behind no scriptures, no doctrine, no church; but they
changed everyone who came in contact with them. Their effect has
not been on the will but on the imagination. They are the avatars of
a religion based on the arts, and in this sense AE is solidly in the
tradition of estheticism. The arts are the expression of the divine imagination, and they act upon us by ennobling our whole nature and
not by giving us maxims for conduct. Vision and intuition finally
lead us into the heavenly path, not the will. Conaire hopes that we
shall finally escape from the body, not by dying but by rising out of
the material into the spiritual like the figure represented by Mark's
sculpture. The bonds of matter will at last wear thin and fall away
until we have excaped into the spirit world.

Felim asks how they will know each other in this condition if no
bodies distinguish one person from another and if they have all
merged into one spirit and one wisdom. However, he answers his
own question when he says that perhaps they will know each other
not by physical but by spiritual characteristics: Rory, by his music;
Paul, by his imaginations; Olive, "as a silver glow with innumerable
stars in it"; Clubborn, by his friendliness. When Olive suggests that
there may be a place where they can meet in the spirit world and
that possibly Paul can show it to them in a vision, Paul tries and
succeeds: "His face was set with intensity of will. He was evoking in
himself memory of a vision. His head turned slightly to one after
another, as one who makes a lit candle to touch with its flame a cir-
cle of unlit candles. There began to glow in each the vision of a vast
hall with high marvellous pillars, a hall lit with a delicate golden
air" (185).

The friends part in the hope that on the following night, Midsummer Eve, when the barriers between heaven and earth are
fragile, they may draw closer to this union which Paul had created
in his vision. As Paul and Olive walk out in the beauty of the night
to commune with the spirit world, they forget each other in their
separate vision; but they are united in their mystic union with the
One. "She was unconscious of the one by her side, and at that moment he loved her more in forgetting than in remembering him"
(188). This anti-Romantic but spiritual ending is typical of AE: The
spirit is stronger than physical attractions, and the idea of the

mystical unity of all souls is more important than the gratification of the reader's usual expectation of a romantic ending with the lovers in an embrace.

As a novelist of the spirit, AE has created in *The Avatars* a new kind of book. Though the plot moves slowly and the transitions are clumsy, the characters are convincing, and their thoughts are sublime. As we have already observed, the idea is more important than the development of plot and character; and AE achieves his full effect in separate passages of luminous beauty. The reader is led into a beautiful world where fine people love each other not for their physical but for their spiritual qualities.

But, in another sense, we cannot call AE a novelist any more than we could consider him a dramatist. Like his poetry, his fiction and his drama have a specific motive—to advance his mystical theories and his spiritual concept of the destiny of mankind in general and of Ireland in particular. Once again, we note the narrow range of his thought and his art, for AE's dominant theme is about the spiritual origin of man and about the inherent powers which are his to use if only he can be made aware of them. This singleness of purpose defines AE's work; and, although he worked in many different areas, his central purpose was always the same: to improve the lot of mankind and to make men aware of their spiritual nature. AE certainly cannot be compared with Yeats in poetry, with O'Casey in drama, or with either E. M. Forster or Conrad in fiction; in artistic ability, they are by far his superior. In the realm of literature, he was more a philosopher than an artist.

CHAPTER 5

AE as Economist:
Co-operation and Nationality

I *Early Pamphlets*

IT may seem strange that a man who was a mystic, a poet, a writer of stories and pseudo-novels, and a painter should also be a newspaper editor, an economist, and a political figure. The picture of AE that emerges is that of a man who lived a *total* life; for he had learned very early that, before a man can be any particular kind of a man or before he can adopt or reject any spiritual attitude or philosophical stance, he must live; and, in order to live, he must satisfy his bodily needs—food, clothing, and shelter. Early in his life, he became an organizer for the Irish Agricultural Organization Society and later the editor of its official organ, *The Irish Homestead.* His political and economic theory was grounded on his mystical foundation, just as his poetry and his fiction were; and he did not hesitate to present his theory in a number of publications—short pamphlets, articles printed in journals, and the full-length book, *The National Being* (1916). This book was the final and definitive statement of his economic theory, and it is perhaps his most widely known book since it has appeared in many translations and in many lands.[1]

The foundation of AE's economic theory was presented in two articles that first appeared in *The Irish Theosophist* in 1897 and that were later reprinted as pamphlets. The first was *The Future of Ireland and the Awakening of the Fires,*[2] a general invocation to the people of Ireland to awaken to their heroic past and to their divine destiny. Basically Romantic in its attack on materialism and industrialism, it seeks the greatness of Ireland in the country's legends and myths. To most Irish people, says AE, freedom means the attempt to be like other nations, to emulate their greatness in industry and mechanization. However, this view does not square with the realities of the times which require noble ideals based on the historical and legendary greatness of Ireland. AE sees the signs of an awakening of the fires in Ireland which have been covered with ashes for centuries.

This theme is AE's familiar philosophy with a nationalistic twist, and it led to an economic theory which affected the economy of Ireland in the years that followed. He concludes the article with an exhortation to the people of Ireland to take up their heroic heritage and make of it an heroic future: "Dear children of Eri, not alone to the past but to to-day belong such destinies. For if you will you may enter the enchanted land: The golden age is all about us, and heroic forms and imperishable love. In that mystic light rolled round our hills and valleys hang deeds and memories that yet live and in-spire. . . . A new cycle is dawning: the sweetness of the morning twilight is in the air. You can breathe it if you will but awaken from your slumber" (10).

A companion piece entitled *Ideals in Ireland: Priest or Hero*[3] was AE's direct attack on the Catholic Church, specifically against the priesthood; for AE felt that this institution was outmoded and was opposed to the heroic ideals he had defended in his first article. Ireland must choose between the priesthood and its ancient heroic culture, which, it should be noted, was a *pagan* culture in the eyes of the Catholic Church. In this work, AE begins with the lines from Walt Whitman which praise the condition of animals ("They do not whine about their condition,/They do not lie awake in the dark and weep for their sins") and those which abjure kneeling ("No one kneels to another, nor to one of his kind that lived thousands of years ago"); and he develops the idea that the priesthood had sup-pressed the divine freedom and creativity of the Irish people.

AE's Transcendental and primitivistic philosophy, which holds that man is good by nature and can be as good as he thinks he is, is obviously at the opposite pole from conventional orthodox Chris-tianity which holds that man is sinful by nature and is redeemed only by the blood of Christ. AE accepted the "beautiful, pathetic and ennobling teachings of Christ," but he could not accept the teaching of institutional Christianity which holds that Christ is divine and that man is base. If Christ is divine, said AE, it is with the essential divinity which exists in all men: "The choice here lies between Priest and Hero as ideal, and I say that whatever is not heroic is not Irish, has not been nourished at the true fountain wherefrom our race and isle derive their mystic fame. There is a life behind the veil, another Eri which the bards knew, singing it as the Land of Immortal Youth. It is not hidden from us, though we have hidden ourselves from it, so that it has become only a fading memory in our hearts and a faery fable upon our lips" (5).

But this condition is to be reversed, said AE, as the imagination of the Gael takes the place of traditional religion. Addressing the priests of Ireland, he says "Soon shall young men, fiery hearted, children of Eri, a new race, roll out their thoughts on the hillsides, before your very doors, O priests, calling your flocks from your dark chapels and twilight sanctuaries to a temple not built with hands, sunlit, starlit, sweet with the odour and incense of earth, from your altars call them to the altars of the hills, soon to be lit up as of old, soon to be the blazing torches of God over the land" (6 - 7).

In all probability, the priests were not terribly frightened by this threat; it was more of a hope than a prediction. But AE was partially right. The fiery-hearted young men did come out carrying torches over the land in the days that lay ahead in the rebellion against England and in the Civil War which followed, but these events were not the kind of rebirth for which AE had hoped. The nationalism that was popular and that caught the imaginations of the young men was rooted in the hatred of England, not in the love of God nor in the remembrance of Ireland's ancient heroic past. Their ideas and ideals went back to Grattan, Tone, and O'Connell—not to Cuchulain.

In *The Building Up of a Rural Civilization* (1910),[4] AE discusses the rural exodus which began after the famine of 1846 and which continued not only in Ireland but throughout the world. He investigates the causes of this exodus and the methods by which it can be stopped, for it must be stopped if civilization is to survive. In this pamphlet AE begins to develop his theory that the country is the basis of civilization, not the town: The country produces everything; the town only manufactures and distributes. The stable and wholesome life of the country relates to the divine through Nature and brings man into communion with the best influences. The problem is, therefore, to make rural life interesting and vital so that the country man will not want to move to the city, to England, or to America.

As to how this change was to be accomplished, AE's answer is the beginning of the program that was to be elaborated in *Co-operation and Nationality* (1912) and *The National Being* (1916): "The business mind of the country must be organized to counter the business mind of the town, the political forces of the farmers must be organized to meet the organized political forces of the towns—and to meet them intelligently" (7). Up to his time, AE felt, the farmer had been exploited because he was not as good a politician as the citydweller. Because the farmer's problem was, first, political, and second, economic, he had to find a way to get legislation passed that was favorable to him without offending the existing political parties, which were divided on the question of Home Rule versus union with Great Britain. Both the Unionist and the Home Ruler must be encouraged to accept agricultural reforms which would aid the farmer.

But political action, though important, was not so important as the ideal which would govern the actions of the cooperative movement. The ideal should be the building up of a true rural civilization, one such as the world had never seen. Such a feat would require first "complete control over the manufacture and sale of all the produce of the countryside . . . " (9). It would mean the consolidation of small cooperatives into general purpose societies. This change would result in greater prosperity for the farmer, which would make rural life more pleasant, stop the rural exodus, and allow farmers and countrymen to exercise a sane voice in the national polity.

II   Co-operation and Nationality

The ideas which had been expressed in these brief early articles and talks were summarized and elaborated upon in *Co-operation and Nationality* which had the subtitle *A Guide for Rural Reformers from this to the Next Generation.*[5] AE begins with the problems of rural life, how to stop the rural exodus, and how to create a rural civilization that is both wholesome and interesting. The civilization that has always flourished in the cities has passed the farmer by: "Civilization in historical times has been a flare-up on a few square miles of brick and mortar. Outside the cities there have always been the same mean houses, the same implements of labour, the same ignorance, want of education, the same oblivion of the finer things in life" (4). As for the way rural civilization can be developed, the farmer must first be able to keep some surplus of wealth beyond the level necessary for mere survival. In order to do so, he must, secondly, organize and exclude the moneylender or gombeen man. In his third chapter, "Need for an Agricultural Revolution," he describes how the farmer is fleeced systematically by dealers through the use of "blockers" and "tanglers." The blockers keep the farmer from bargaining with other dealers until the one they work for is ready for the farmer to sell at the dealer's price. The tangler, a variation of the blocker, has the task of confusing the farmer so that he will not know the true worth of his produce and will accept a lower price than he desires. The agricultural revolution that AE envisioned would give the farmer control not only of production but of distribution and would thereby eliminate the middle man. Because the farmer would become prosperous, he could then afford the niceties of life which lead to an interesting rural civilization.

The cooperation which AE advocated should not be confused with Socialism; he saw no indication that Ireland, and certainly not the rural areas, would yield to Socialism: "An Irish farmer would pour down boiling lead on the emissaries of the state who tried to nationalize his land, the land he sweated sixty years to pay for" (23). Since in his view the land reform which had made the tenants proprietors had precluded this possibility, the danger was not from the state but from the gombeen man who would become the land-owner if not checked by the cooperative movement, the only organization that could stop him. In fact, AE distrusted the state as an abstraction which stifles human values and human initiative, as we have already seen in *The Interpreters.* However, he did fear that the power of the state might gain a hold on the farmer through its efforts to help him: " . . . Without State socialism we may yet get worship of the state, and belief in its powers, developed to such an extent that the community will place itself completely in the hands of the government to the utter destruction of self-reliance, in-itiative, and independence of spirit" (25 - 26). To AE, Sir Horace Plunkett had, through his creation of the cooperative movement, led Ireland away from "Westminsterism" or excessive reliance on the state. He was able to bring together the most diverse kinds of Irishmen—Orangeman and Fenian, Church of Ireland and Catholic clergymen, Ulster Unionist and Munster Nationalist—and to re-main nonpolitical in his effort to unite Ireland in the cooperative movement.

Cooperation was the means to an improved social order in which all men would cooperate and replace ruthless competition with mutual aid, bring town and country into a mutually dependent society, and benefit both farmer and merchant. AE believed that a man is not fully human until he senses this cooperative need: "Wherever there is mutual aid, wherever there is constant give and take, wherever the prosperity of the individual depends directly and obviously on the prosperity of the community about him, there the social order tends to produce fine types of character, with a devotion to public ideas; and this is the real object of all government" (34). But, where men are isolated from each other and ruthlessly compete for wealth, the Devil is at work, and the body politic suffers.

To AE, laissez-faire individualism leads to the destruction of both man and society: "Isolate your man from obligations to a social order and in most cases his soul drops into the pit like a rotten apple from the Tree of Life. Fine character in a race is evolved and not taught" (34 - 35). Historically, Ireland had not had a real social order of this kind since the time of the clans when clansmen and chiefs had had a mutual relationship under which both profited. The clansman had worked for the aristocracy, and it had protected the clansman. But, under the English Ascendency, where the aristocracy simply drew rent, this relationship left no true social order but created merely a commercial relationship.

AE did not desire to return to this feudal form of society, for he realized that life had to go forward and that times were different than they had been under the clans. But the principle of cooperation had remained as valid as in those days, and AE's main principle was that a social order must have three main goals: economic development, political stability, and a desirable social life. The cooperatives had already begun to accomplish these ends: dairy societies had given the farmer control of the manufacture and sale of butter, credit societies had made it possible for him to borrow money at reasonable rates of interest, and cooperative stores made it possible for him to buy commodities of a good quality at wholesale prices. Until this time, the farmer had been forced to buy at retail prices and to sell at wholesale prices—a system under which few businesses could survive very long.

Protecting the farmers against inflation was another effect of the cooperatives. The workers in the town needed cheap food, and their employers had either to raise wages or find cheaper food. The choice was obvious: employers flooded the towns with produce, reduced prices, and helped their workers at the expense of the farmers. Agriculture was, not only the basic form of human work, but the most vulnerable to such unfair tactics; despite its great importance as " . . . the basic human occupation. Let it fail, and humanity must disappear, and the birds of the air and the beasts of the field war for lordship of the planet. Our princes and captains of industry, and all they control, the high-built factories and titanic mills, might all disappear without man disappearing; but cut away man from the fields and fruits of the earth and in six months there will be silence in the streets, and in half a century the forests will be butting at London and leaning their shoulders against the houses to overwhelm them" (40). Many people failed to realize this obvious fact, and in the towns the opposition to the cooperative movement was strongest. AE calls these towns "arid patches of humanity" with "mental bogs about them," and he compares them to Tyre and Sidon, the decadent cities of ancient Phoenicia. Therefore, the town had to be brought into the cooperative movement for the good of both town and country.

At this time, AE did not object to Home Rule, nor did he think it very important. It really did not matter whether Ireland was a part of the British Empire or not. The true basis of nationality was not the political organizations which debated Home Rule and Unionism; it was, instead, cooperative and productive ventures. AE felt that the three movements which had done the most for Ireland in recent times had been the cooperative movement, the Gaelic League, and the Industrial Development Associations. The cooperative movement was showing farmers how to improve the quality of their lives by establishing a sound economic base for that occupation. The Gaelic League was developing ideals of national culture by reuniting the people with their ancient heritage. And the Industrial Development Associations, which aided in the development of new factories and mills, were doing the same thing for industry that the cooperative movement was doing for the farmer.

But all of these actions and organizations would be in vain unless a form of democracy developed which would establish an aristocracy of talent to replace the politics of the demogogue. A good society would only result from a cooperative enterprise in which citizens worked together for the greater good rather than for their own individual interests. The Cooperative Commonwealth, therefore, was the only viable alternative to either state Socialism or capitalism. It alone allowed for the development of personal genius and unhampered local initiative, and it was the only answer to the industrial anarchy which then prevailed in Western Europe.

AE's whole philosophy as it relates to society is summarized in this statement: "The object of all religion, art, literature and economics is the creation of perfect human beings. Religion aims at making the perfect human being by acting on man's spiritual nature. Art aims at making the perfect human being by acting on his aesthetic nature; literature by acting on his intelligent nature; while economics aims at perfecting humanity by using material means and agencies" (63).

The perfection of human nature also included women, who, according to AE, had been excluded from a voice in the affairs of the nation. For years, women had been doing the work of men on the farms; it had made them old before their time; it had made them want to leave the farm and even to leave Ireland. Women were needed not only to produce strong healthy children and to provide homes for them, but to redeem life from its crudeness. In a passage that reminds us of Bernard Shaw's concept of the Life Force embodied in women, AE describes what women can add to Irish life:

Men are at once abstract and gross, and the poles of their nature are more apart than a woman's. Men can dream of heavens and principalities and powers and yet be beasts, and between their abstract ideals and their gross occupations lies a desert where life has been neglected in Ireland; and that has been because the voice of women, the cherisher of life above all things, has been unheard in the national councils. What women, the best women, are concerned with is the character of life. They love strength, health, vitality, kindness. They desire to see the comfortable home, the strong man coming in and out, great sons and the laughter and roundness of well-nourished children. Women are the preservers of life, and because they have had no organized life or union of their own, because they were unable to make known their desires and needs, life has decayed in Ireland. (70)

The society known as The United Irishwomen was formed in 1910 to supply this need and to remedy neglect of the women of Ireland. This movement became a necessary component in the formation of national policy. Once again, AE was ahead of his time as one of the first advocates of "women's liberation."

III   The National Being

In the years between 1912 and 1916, much happened in Ireland; and AE continued to write about the economic and political issues of the day, with such short works as *The Rural Community* (1913), *Oxford University and the Cooperative Movement* (1914), *Ireland,*

Agriculture and the War (1915), and *Talks with an Irish Farmer*
(1916). But his greatest work in this area was *The National Being*,
which appeared in 1916.[6] After decades of fruitless attempts to
secure freedom for Ireland, the Third Home Rule Bill had finally
passed the British Parliament in 1914. Because of World War I, the
bill was temporarily set aside since Great Britain did not want a
hostile or even a neutral Ireland that was so close to her own shores
to be available as a base for enemy agents. But, since AE was
hopeful that the bill would finally be implemented, he anticipates
in *The National Being* an Irish Free State which he hopes will
develop in the years to come—one that looks back to its ancient
origins in myth and legend and ahead to its future as a modern
European state. The "national being" is the soul of the race, the nation is the body that contains that soul, and civilization is the exter-
nalization of the soul and character of the race. The job ahead is to
create that body and soul and that outward appearance of the two
by which the nation is known to other nations. This is a task similar
to that which the German thinkers, scientists, poets, philosophers,
and historians did for Germany; but AE hopes that the result will be
more like what the Greek thinkers did for Greece in ancient times,
instead of the militarism of Germany.

The national life of Ireland, said AE, is too materialistic; and the
people are more governed by passion than by thought. But, since
Ireland has a new opportunity, it should create a nation which will
reflect her ancient and great tradition. What is wrong with Ireland
is also what is wrong with all modern states: they are no longer
guided by the Oversoul or the spirit of the race; and their leaders
lack greatness. AE does not know what has caused this degenera-
tion; perhaps it is a result of the decline in modern literature, the
decline of epic greatness. None of the great heroes—Cuchulain,
Hector, Theseus, Arjuna, for example—have found their counter-
parts in modern times. This same Romantic retrospective tendency
we have already seen in AE's poetry and stories; for his literary efforts were, in part, designed to fill in this gap in modern literature.

Much of what AE says in *The National Being* repeats what he
had said previously in *Co-operation and Nationality*. Although the
need for agriculture, and for the cooperative movement had been
covered, he develops some ideas such as the necessity for the
organization of farm labor. But the main difference between the
two books is that, in the time that had intervened, AE had seen the
Dublin Strike of 1913, the beginning of World War I, and growing

rebelliousness in Ireland. He was now more interested in the plight of the industrial worker than he had been in 1913, and this book reveals that change of attitude. He feels that the industrial worker has been treated badly and that there was a great disparity between his spiritual birthright and his life on earth. In church, such a worker was told that he was the son of God, that he had an immortal soul, and that Heaven awaited him after death. But, on Monday, he was again a slave, who had to depend on the ruthless whim of his employer. What concerned AE was that the worker had no rights, was not a part of the economy, but was merely a tool to be exploited, and the schools only conditioned him to accept this fate.

Labor in Ireland, says AE, is opposed by the press, the law, the police, and even sometimes by the clergy. The only hope for labor lies in its own strength. Strikes are useless, he says, as the cost of increased wages are only passed on to the consumer, and the cost of his raise is eventually passed on to the laborer in the form of higher prices. "Capital is like a ship which, however the tide rises or falls, floats upon it, and is not sunken more deeply in the water at high tide than at low tide" (77 - 78). The only hope was for labor to attract the same kind of intelligence to its cause that capital attracted. The emancipation of labor, he feels, would not come through revolution but through evolution; and this evolution would come about through experience, intellect, and desire.

In comparing the situation of the farmer and the city laborer, AE pointed out that, while the farmers were for the most part free but unorganized, the city laborers were neither free *nor* organized. Of the two, the farmer was in the better position since his subsistence was to some extent assured. But both could help themselves by organizing and cooperating with each other. Since strikes, political action, and revolution were doomed to fail because of the superior strength of capital and its hold on society, farmer and laborer could control through their cooperation both production and distribution and could therefore cut out the capitalist who controlled distribution and who made a profit without any real labor on his part. The major problem, therefore, was to redirect profits so as to assure workers and farmers of a guaranteed income, regular subsistence, and a pleasant life. The cooperative movement could not only accomplish this status but could also habituate men toward a harmonious social life based on cooperation instead of competition. In order to accomplish these ends, AE advocated the direct sale through cooperatives of food by farmers to the city laborers. The workers would establish these cooperatives in the cities for the purpose of such direct sale.

AE did not advocate making the cooperative way of life compulsory, nor did he insist upon it as the only way of life, but he did believe that it was the only hope for Ireland at that time. He saw little or no hope for reforms initiated by governments, since they were not responsive enough to the will of the people, particularly in large countries, and were too much under the control of wealthy persons. He believed with Rousseau that the general will tends toward the good, but it is thwarted by the state, the press, and the banks. Since all of these institutions and all agencies of distribution are controlled by capital, a group of a few hundred men united in a cooperative could exert enough force to develop their own means of production and distribution.

Another aspect of *The National Being* not found in *Co-operation and Nationality* was concerned with the ideal form of government for Ireland. AE, who was opposed to the importation of English representative government, had definite ideas as to what the new government should be like. His main objection to British government was that it tended too much toward compromise; and, when a compromise was reached, too often the right course of action was forgotten or neglected. The ideal government for Ireland, he felt, should have two representative assemblies. The first, the general assembly or parliament, "should be elected by counties or cities to deal with general interests, taxation, justice, education, the duties and rights of individual citizens as citizens" (114 - 15). The second assembly would consist of specific organized bodies or committees elected by the persons who were involved in specific occupations: farmers, laborers, professional men. These specialists would be responsible for their own areas of concern, and they would insure the consideration of expert knowledge in solving the problems of the nation. The alternative to this proposed group would be to run the risk of incompetent persons being appointed or elected to positions that required technical or expert knowledge.

It was important for AE that Ireland have a government which would be consistent with its national character. Every nation has its own national character; in ancient Greece, it was the idea of beauty; in recent Germany, the concept of power had prevailed. Although Ireland had not been free to pursue its own national tendency for centuries, the powerful and original Irish characteristic was a combination of democracy and aristocracy. The ancient clans were aristocratic in leadership, but they were economically democratic in that the land belonged to the clan as a whole and not to a powerful leader.[7] This tendency had been reversed in Ireland in recent times:

Instead of being democratic in our economic life, with the aristocracy of character and intelligence to lead us, we became meanly individualistic in our economics and meanly democratic in leadership. That is, we allowed individualism—the devilish doctrine of every man for himself—to be the keynote of our economic life; where, above all things, the general good and not the enrichment of the individual should be considered. For our leaders we chose energetic, commonplace types, and made them represent us in the legislature; though it is in leadership above all that we need, not the aristocracy of birth, but the aristocracy of character, intellect, and will. (126 - 27)

This idea has already appeared in Chapter 3, for in "The Iron Age" he wrote that "We choose the chieftains of our race/From hucksters in the market place." For the most part, he believed, Ireland had not chosen her leaders well; but, when an aristocratic person like Charles Stuart Parnell had been chosen, Ireland had responded with love and respect.

The last part of *The National Being* deals with military affairs, conscription, and foreign relations. AE does not see Ireland as becoming a great power in terms of military strength; moreover, to become such a military power is not even desirable nor the best way to achieve national unity. Military strength not only makes the state harsh and cruel but creates the same condition in its enemies. AE is ready to admit, however, that society has not found a more efficient way of uniting a people. In wartime, under the influence of military discipline, men learn to be brave and endure hardships, wounds, and even death. The great problem is how to apply this lesson to peaceful purposes, and AE's faith was that the cooperative movement would do so. He even suggested in this book a form of peaceful conscription: young men would give two years of their lives to the state for peaceful and constructive work instead of learning the destructive work of a wartime army. Such cooperative effort would create a real citizenry in place of the usual collection of individuals who were fighting about or for mean objectives. "The greatest problem of all civilizations," he wrote, "is the creation of citizens: that is, of people who are dominated by the ideal of the general welfare, who will sink private desire and work harmoniously with their fellow-citizens for the highest good of their race" (136).

To AE, war was a fact of modern as well as of ancient life, and all nations have required armies to defend themselves against their enemies. AE's basic assumption concerning war and international relations is that war is the result of hatred in the soul of man. It is not national leaders alone who bring nations to war; they could not do so unless the people were ready for war. Hatred begets hatred. Writing of the hatred of Irish Nationalists for England, AE says: "Race hatred is the cheapest and basest of all national passions, and it is the nature of hatred, as it is the nature of love, to change us into the likeness of that which we contemplate. We grow nobly like what we adore, and ignobly like what we hate; and no people in Ireland became so anglicized in intellect and temperament, and even in the manner of expression, as those who hated our neighbors most" (150).

Referring to the enmity between Ulster[8] and the South of Ireland over Home Rule, he writes:

Nations hate other nations for the evil which is in themselves; but they are as little given to self-analysis as individuals, and while they are right to overcome evil, they should first try to understand the genesis of the passion in their own nature. If we understand this, many of the ironies of history will be intelligible. We will understand why it was that our countrymen in Ulster and our countrymen in the rest of Ireland, who have denounced each other so vehemently, should at last appear to have exchanged characteristics: why in the North, having passionately protested against physical force movements, no-rent manifestos, and contempt for Imperial Parliament, they should have come themselves at last to organize a physical force movement, should threaten to pay no taxes, and should refuse obedience to an Act of Parliament. We will understand also why it was their opponents came themselves to address to Ulster all the arguments and denunciations Ulster had addressed to them. (151 - 52)

The Act of Parliament referred to was the Third Home Rule Bill that had been passed by the British Parliament and resisted by the Ulster Volunteers. The Irish Volunteers were organized in the South to counteract this anti-Home Rule movement, and this enmity is what AE refers to in the passage above.

Since AE felt that Ireland was too small and too weak to achieve national unity through military aggression, the only possible way to such an achievement was through peace and cooperation. If Ireland could find peace at home, she would probably find it with her neighbors; and the result of cooperation would be a friendlier spirit on the part of Ireland toward the rest of the world, which AE felt would be reciprocated by other nations. Not only would such a situation be helpful to Ireland, but it would also point the way toward the peaceful settlement of international disputes.

It seemed inevitable to AE that individuals in modern society would be increasingly dominated by the state and more closely united into national organizations. For this reason, it was most important that the nation should have concern for the individual. The fact that people yield to the demands of the state, even give their lives for it, indicates a subconscious drive toward national unity:

For what do they die unless the spirit in man has some inner certitude that the divine event to which humanity tends is a unity of its multitudinous life, and that a State—even a bad State—must be preserved by its citizens, because it is at least an attempt at organic unity? It is a simulacrum of the ideal; it contains the germ or possibility of that to which the spirit of man is travelling. It disciplines the individual in service to that greater being in which it will find its fulfilment, and a bad State is better than no State at all. To be without a State is to prowl backward from the divinity before us to the beast behind us. (160)

The tendency toward nationality is spiritual and comes from the divine world, and its aim is the creation of a natural world which more closely resembles the spirit world. AE's nationalism becomes metaphysical since he relates human energy to the overall divine plan for the world. Freedom and the long march toward human liberty did not happen by accident; they were and are the fulfillment of the divine purpose:

I believe profoundly that men do not hold the ideas of liberty or solidarity, which have moved them so powerfully, merely as phantasies which are pleasant to the soul or make ease for the body; but because, whether they struggle passionately for liberty or to achieve a solidarity, in working for these two ideals, which seem in conflict, they are divinely supported, in unison with the divine nature, and energies as real as those the scientist studies—as electricity, as magnetism, heat or light—do descend into the soul and reinforce it with elemental energy. We are here for the purposes of soul, and there can be no purpose in individualizing the soul if essential freedom is denied to it and there is only a destiny. Wherever essential freedom, the right of the spirit to choose its own heroes and its own ideals, is denied, nations rise in rebellion. But the spirit in man is wrought in a likeness to Deity, which is that harmony and unity of Being which upholds the universe; and by the very nature of the spirit, while it asserts its

freedom, its impulses lead it to a harmony with all life, to a solidarity or
brotherhood with it. (162 - 63)

Could it be that here AE was already justifying the Irish rebellion
that was in the making? It certainly seems that his support of it is the
point of reference in the preceding passage—a metaphysical
justification for the right of revolution. Though he himself was not a
revolutionary and though he rejected violence as a means of
political change, AE makes the assertion that it happens when "the
right of the spirit to choose its own heroes and its own ideals" is
denied. AE, like the prophet of old, warned his contemporaries and
attempted to give his society insight into its motives, its purposes,
and its destiny. He had about as much success as most prophets
have had, and Ireland had to go through the troubles ahead before
the partition could finally bring a temporary peace to the country.

The National Being concludes with an appeal to all of the
spiritual leaders of Ireland—the clergy, the poets, the writers, and
the thinkers—for help in changing the life of Ireland from the com-
petitive to the cooperative model. AE once again reviews the ancient heritage of Ireland, rooted in the myths and legends of her
past, and affirms the importance of national policy at this historical
moment: "To quicken the intellect and imagination of Ireland, to
co-ordinate our economic life for the general good, should be the
objects of national policy, and will subserve the evolutionary purpose" (166). He felt that the artist would create the ideal image of
Irish life but that the state would finally determine the fate of its
people. That fate would be mean if the state became a tyranny, but
it could be noble if the work of building the state was done rightly.
The great task of government in Europe and in Ireland was to
create a harmonious life for the people, but such harmony could
only come from within the souls of the people who composed the
nations; it could not be imposed from without.

Although Oliver St. John Gogarty called AE an "angelic
anarchist,"[9] he was not entirely correct. AE was not an Anarchist, as
we have seen, for he held firm beliefs about the necessity of the nation and its divine origin. What he objected to strongly was the
tyrannical state which would deprive its members of the liberty to
seek their own destiny. Other, more apt names for AE would be a
"heavenly economist," a "metaphysical nationalist," or a "spiritual
politician." But, in the end, all labels fail with AE; he was simply a
man who was seeking the destiny and the true spiritual nature of
man.

CHAPTER 6

AE as Statesman:
"the politics of time"

I The Dublin Strike

THE period from 1913 to 1922 was a troubled, confused, and baffling time for AE since Ireland was troubled by a series of events which caused him much anguish and required him to take sides in the disputes of the times. In *The Interpreters*, he had written about "the politics of time and the politics of eternity"; he was much more at ease with the politics of eternity—those metaphysical principles that he had expressed in his writings. However, the events of the period forced him to take an active part in the politics of time; some of the occurrences that affected him deeply during these years were the Dublin Strike of 1913, the passage of the Home Rule Bill and its subsequent postponement, the Easter Rising of 1916, the failure of the Home Rule Convention of 1917, the concurrent ascendency of the Sinn Fein and the formation of the Irish Republic, the Anglo-Irish War, and finally the Civil War over the Anglo-Irish Treaty, which gave Southern Ireland the status of a free state. During "the Troubles," World War I was going on in the background; and Ireland was a reluctant ally of Britain. While some Irishmen were fighting voluntarily with the British in Irish regiments, other Irishmen were plotting with the Germans to defeat England.

But AE lived in the world of time; though he occasionally visited the world of eternity, he know that he had to play his part in the tragedy being enacted. Until 1913, he had, for the most part stayed out of politics while working with the Irish Agricultural Organization Society to extend cooperation in Ireland. In 1913, however, his sympathy for the workers of the city of Dublin was aroused by the Dublin Strike and the lockout of the workers by their employers.

Fired by the injustic shown by these employers who refused to deal
with the laborers unless they agreed to remain out of the labor unions, AE wrote and spoke on behalf of labor. His pamphlet, *The
Dublin Strike*,[1] is composed of three parts, the first of which was a
speech given by AE in the Royal Albert Hall in London on
November 1, 1913. With cutting irony and stinging invective, he
accused the employers of a failure of sympathy and understanding
and of an unwillingness to negotiate. After a vivid description of the
slums in which the workers lived and of their extreme desperation,
he offered this prophetic statement: "The labour uprising in Dublin
is the despairing effort of humanity to raise itself out of a dismal
swamp of disease and poverty."

The second part of the pamphlet is an open letter addressed to
the employers which had appeared before the Albert Hall speech[2]
in the *Irish Times* on October 7, 1913. Entitled "To the Masters of
Dublin," whom AE calls "the Shylocks of industry," he warns the
employers in this open letter that times are changing and that their
actions will arouse a power which they do not yet full comprehend—the sleeping power of Irish labor. He calls the employers
uncultivated, incompetent, arrogant, and "bad citizens" who,
though wealthy, contributed nothing to the city of Dublin. He ac-
cuses them of misusing their power, and he warns them that they
will pay the price of this misuse: "You may succeed in your policy
and ensure your own damnation by your victory. The men whose
manhood you have broken will loathe you, and will always be
brooding and scheming to strike a fresh blow. The children will be
taught to curse you. The infant being moulded in the womb will
have breathed into its starved body the vitality of hate." (6) This
statement may have been true, it certainly was sincere, but it failed
in its rhetorical purpose; for, as we might guess, the employers were
not moved.

The third part of *The Dublin Strike* appeared first in the *London
Times* on November 13, 1913, after being refused by the Dublin
press. It is called, in its reprinted form, *The Tragedy of Labour in
Dublin*. Here AE says that he has addressed the masters of Dublin
in vain, that they simply do not comprehend the forces with which
they are dealing, and that they do not comprehend his role: "I am
charged with being a revolutionary, I who for seven or eight years
past have week by week been expounding an orderly evolution of
society. I am charged as being against religion, I the sole poet of my
generation who has never written a single poem which did not try to

express a spiritual mood."[3] Despite such charges, AE once again warns of impending doom in these significant and prophetic words: "Dublin seems to be stumbling darkly and blindly to a tragedy, and the silence of those who foresee and do not speak is a crime. It is time for the Chorus to cry out to warn the antagonists in the drama."[4]

Ironically, this pamphlet sold for only one penny, but AE's advice might have prevented disaster had his views been heeded. For it seems likely that the Dublin Strike—or "The Larkin Labour War," as T. A. Jackson calls it—led to the Easter Rising of 1916, to the resurgence of Sinn Fein, and to the Troubles. For the "army" of the Transport Union, composed of men who guarded the platform against police during strike meetings, became the Citizen's Army; and this army in time joined forces with the Irish Volunteers to provide the force which finally broke the hold of British rule in Ireland.[5] James Connolly, one of the sixteen men who were executed as leaders of the 1916 Easter Rising, was a labor union leader, chief of the Transport Union, Commander of the Citizen's Army, and editor of *The Irish Worker*.[6] Clearly, the seeds of the revolution were sown in 1913; and AE was wise enough to foresee the impending tragedy in which the dissatifaction of Irish labor merged with the discontent of those who were working for Irish independence.

II *The Troubles*

AE's correspondence at this time also reveals his premonition of the troubles to come. In a letter written October 14, 1914, to his old friend and correspondent Charles Weekes, he says: "I have a conviction deep inside me that we are going to have one more heart-searching trial, baring our lives to the very spirit, and that within the next few years."[7] When the revolt came on Easter Monday, April 24, 1916, AE recognized it as the beginning of the troubles he had anticipated. That he attributed it to the Dublin Strike of 1913 is made clear in his letter of August 18, 1916,[8] to Weekes:

Personally I believe there would have been no revolt if the employers and authorities had not been so unmerciful and unjust during the great strike. They left labour inflamed. I wrote then a letter, suppressed here, but which appeared in *The Times* [London] in which I said "if the authorities were wanting to make Dublin a place with bombs blazing in the street they were going the right way about it." It was labour supplied the personal element in the revolt. It had a real grievance. The cultural element, poets, Gaels, etc. never stir more than one per cent of a country. It is only when economic injustice stirs the workers that they unite their grievance with all other grievances. The stirring element in this was labour.

AE was right, for the alliance of Connolly's Citizen Army with the Irish Republican Brotherhood brought about the Easter Rising of 1916.[9]

In 1925, AE quoted Rabindranath Tagore, the Indian poet, in *The Irish Statesman* as saying that "The complete man must never be sacrificed to the patriotic man." Ireland, AE asserted, had often asked its men to sacrifice their humanity in the interest of patriotism: "How often in Ireland have we not been asked to sacrifice our complete humanity, beauty, love, justice, as an offering to patriotism? . . . It is a bad patriotism which demands from us the sacrifice of things which are higher than itself."[10] Only two years before the Easter Rising of 1916, AE had written to Plunkett to object to a speech in Tipperary in which Plunkett had spoken in favor of Home Rule. AE's objection to that speech was based on his belief that cooperation was nonpolitical and that to support Home Rule would jeopardize the nonpolitical nature of the cooperative movement.[11] But, during the Troubles, AE wrote an admiring poem about the men who had taken part in the Easter Rising; and he later supported the men of Sinn Fein in their decision to remain aloof from the Home Rule Convention of 1917.

Only a very strong man could remain neutral in those troubled days, and AE was not that strong. The poem that he wrote about the men who had died for Ireland in the Easter Rising was entitled "Salutation," but he did not include it in *Collected Poems* which may indicate that he did not find it of lasting value. However, although he felt at the time the necessity of showing his admiration for the men who died for Ireland, the first stanza shows his divided feeling:

> Their dream had left me numb and cold
> But yet my spirit rose in pride,
> Refashioning in burnished gold
> The images of those who died
> Or were shut in the penal cell.
> Here's to you, Pearse, your dream not mine,
> But yet the thought for this you fell
> Has turned life's waters into wine.[12]

In spite of AE's feelings against excessive patriotism and partisan politics, he took part in the Irish Home Rule Convention which met for the first time on July 25, 1917, in Dublin. His view of the situation is expressed in "Thoughts for a Convention," first printed in the *Irish Times* on May 26, 28, and 29, 1917.[13] Though he was reluctant to take a political stance, AE believed that the urgency of the conflict was so great that no Irishman could afford to remain aloof. He had to contribute whatever knowledge and skill he had in helping the conflicting parties reach an agreement. This agreement, he said, must first be between the three Irish parties involved—the Unionists, Sinn Fein[14] and the Constitutional Nationalists—and then between Ireland and Great Britain. Since it was necessary to understand the position of each of these Irish parties in order to understand the conflict, he began his treatment with a very clear and impartial anaylsis of the three parties and their differences. The fact that this essay was printed in *The Irish Home-Rule Convention*, published in New York, indicates that AE must have had in mind an audience that was not exclusively Irish.

The Unionists, said AE, are descendants of settlers from England and Scotland; though they love Ireland, they retain habits, beliefs, and traditions which distinguish them from the Irish of Gaelic origin.[15] Economically, the more powerful people of Ireland, the Unionists, who live in Ulster, Ireland's northern industrial region, possess "openness and energy of character, great organizing power, and a mastery over materials. . . " (101). They believe their prosperity is due largely to the Union, and that this prosperity would be lessened by a separation from Great Britain. The Unionists fear that an Irish legislature in Dublin would be dominated by small farmers of the South who might have little or no knowledge of the needs of Ulster industry or international trade. Furthermore, Unionists fear that they would be oppressed by the Catholic majority in Southern Ireland. Thus their differences are based on differing origins, division of interest between agriculture and industry, and religious differences. The South tends to be predominantly agricultural, Gaelic, and Catholic; while the North tends to be mainly industrial, Scotch-English, and Protestant. The Unionists are convinced that no small country can be really independent; an independent Ireland would be the focus of international intrigue hostile to Great Britain and, therefore, hostile to them. Accordingly, security for Ireland and prosperity for all could best be preserved by the Union.

The Sinn Fein party represents the spiritual heirs of the ancient Gaelic race in Ireland: "They regard the preservation of their nationality as a sacred charge, themselves as a conquered people owing no allegiance to the dominant race" (103 - 04). Sinn Fein does not see itself as traitorous to the British Empire when its members struggle for independence because they have never accepted it as their nation. AE does not mention the word *blood;* obviously the Gaelic blood has been diluted by intermarriage with other national groups such as the Anglo-Saxon, the Norman, the Norse, and the Scottish. Theirs is a *spiritual* heritage, but it is nonetheless strong because of this fact: "They are inspired by an ancient history, a literature stretching beyond the Christian era, a national culture and distinct national ideals which they desire to manifest in a civilization which shall not be an echo or imitation of any other" (104).[16] This party is clearly opposed to the Union because Sinn Fein members "assert that the Union kills the soul of the people; that empires do not permit the intensive cultivation of human life: that they destroy the richness and variety of existence by the extinction of peculiar and unique gifts, and the substitution therefor of a culture which has its value mainly for the people who created it, but is as alien to our race as the mood of the scientist is to the artist or poet" (106).

These first two parties are diametrically opposed to each other, but the third party, the Constitutional Nationalist, occupies a middle position in the struggle. Its members have tried at the same time to maintain the connection of Ireland with the British Empire and to work for Home Rule in administration and legislation. Since the Constitutional Nationalists have taken this middle position, they have been attacked by the other two parties and their sincerity has been questioned. But, because the Nationalists have been more practical than the other two parties, most of the reforms since the Union are to their credit. Since this party has been most successful in improving the quality of life in Ireland, it has had the greatest following. But, owing to recent events such as the 1916 Easter Rising, they no longer have this following: "The intellect of Ireland is now fixed on fundamentals, and the compromise this middle party is able to offer does not make provision for the ideals of either of the extremists, and indeed meets little favour anywhere in a country excited by recent events in world history, where revolutionary changes are expected and a settlement far more in accord with fundamental principles" (108). Although AE does not say so, he probably found this third party most congenial to his own thought and disposition.

A letter dated June 1, 1916, to A. J. Balfour, the Foreign Secretary of Great Britain,[17] indicated his belief that three conditions must be met in order to insure peace in Ireland: (1) Ireland must be united and self-governing. (2) Ireland must be friendly to Great Britain. (3) Ulster must have a guarantee against oppression of its religious and economic interests.[18] This letter seems to be the basis of his proposed solution offered in "Thoughts for a Convention."

AE believed that the partition of Ireland into North and South would not work and that it would sow the seeds of domestic strife for decades to come. Any settlement which would not satisfy all of the parties in Ireland would be a waste of effort and would be doomed to failure. AE must have been looking ahead to recent developments in Northern Ireland when he wrote these prophetic words:

I have no doubt that if Ireland was granted the essential freedom and wholeness in its political life it desires, its mood also would be turned. I have no feelings of race hatred, no exultation in thought of the downfall of any race; but as a close observer of the mood of millions in Ireland, I feel certain that if their claim is not met they will brood and scheme and wait to strike a blow; though the dream may be handed on from them to their children and their children's children, yet they will hope, sometime, to give the last vengeful thrust of enmity at the stricken heart of the empire. (128)

AE still believed that Home Rule was possible, that Ireland could have dominion status, but that she could control her own taxation and trade policy. These powers were not included in the Third Home Rule Bill then pending, but he felt that they should be incorporated in the final treaty.

"Thoughts for a Convention" concludes with a strong plea to Ulster to cooperate in a self-governing, united Ireland; and AE gives strong arguments in favor of such cooperation. He feels that the fears of oppression from Southern Ireland are groundless, that Ulster would be free to do all of the things it had done before the passage of a Home Rule Bill, and that Ulster was so strong, that it would probably dominate all of Ireland economically and industrially. Though not really necessary, Ulster would certainly be justified in asking for certain safeguards such as a civil service commission to insure fair competition for government posts and guarantees of local control over local administration. But the national situation would be far better if the entire country could cooperate in such a way that the old division would be forgotten. Ireland would still cooperate with Great Britain in matters of defense, but conscription would be the prerogative of the Irish parliament, and the supplying of army and navy posts and bases would be the function of the local governments. The idea would be to keep local resources in Ireland instead of exporting money to England. When money left the country, wage earners must follow it; and this exodus led to depopulation.

The program that AE proposed in "Thoughts for a Convention" is sensible, fair, and would have paved the way for a successful compromise; but the Convention, suggested by Lloyd George as a possible alternative to the Home Rule Bill, was doomed from the start. Even had England agreed to give Ireland her freedom, it would have been impossible for the Irish to agree as to the right method. The first meeting of the Convention was held on July 25, 1917; concurrently, all Irish prisoners in England were released and returned to Ireland as a gesture of faith and good will. But other party developments and problems prevented acceptance of this gesture and the success of the Convention. When the prisoners landed at Dun Laoghaire, the Sinn Fein flags were flying. Moreover, Sinn Fein refused to take any part in the Convention; it had its own plans for freedom; Sinn Fein candidates were beginning to win seats in the House of Commons; and its members were now planning an Irish Republic.

Other problems doomed the Convention from the start. Lloyd George's ambiguous attitude toward the Convention indicated his feeling that the whole affair was only a political expedient. Second, the extreme parties did not wholeheartedly support the Convention. Sinn Fein refused to take part, as we have observed; and the Ulster Unionists were committed to consult with Sir Edward Carson and the Ulster government before agreeing to any solution. When the final report was adopted by a vote of 44 to 29, with many abstentions, the Convention was somewhat short of the "substantial agreement" that had been established by Lloyd George as a condition for accepting its report. Ironically, the vote on the report caused a permanent split between the Southern Unionists, who began to accept the idea of Home Rule, and the Ulster Unionists, who opposed it to the end. The report was lost sight of in the next crisis, which was conscription for Ireland.[19]

AE sensed the futility of the Convention long before it was over. The last meeting of the Convention was held on April 5, 1918, and AE had sent Sir Horace Plunkett a letter offering his resignation on February 1. His main reason for resigning was that he felt the Convention could not succeed in its purpose as long as the delegates from Northern Ireland were not free to negotiate and were hampered by their pledge to consult Belfast before acting on any proposal. Also, he doubted whether the British government would submit the report of the Convention to a vote of the Irish people and without such a privilege the report would have no force.[20] When Plunkett replied to AE from London, he asked him to reconsider, and expressed hope that the British government would give effect to the results of the Convention.[21] AE replied saying that he could not comply with Plunkett's request.

By this time, AE had come to the conclusion that the time for compromise was past and that Nationalism would have to run its course. On February 3, he wrote to Sir Horace: "I am very sorry I cannot do as you suggest. I have come to the conclusion that the Convention, constituted as it is, is simply an obstacle to an Irish settlement, and that the only thing to do is to let the new forces of Nationalism manifest themselves in their full strength. I think, in spite of South Armagh, that they will grow stronger and I think nothing but the most determined opposition to British Government in Ireland will have any effect on that Government."

AE believed there never was any hope in the Convention—that the British politicians, Lord Asquith, Bonar Law, and Lloyd George, had conspired with Sir Edward Carson to oppose any inclusion of Ulster in an Irish Home Rule government. Furthermore, AE feared that his efforts on behalf of the Convention would interfere with and jeopardize his work in the Irish Agricultural Organization Society. His letter to Plunkett concludes with the strongest words he had yet written in favor of Nationalism: "The Sinn Feiners were right in their intuitions from the first. If I had followed my intuition from the first I would have remained away also. A man must be either an Irishman or an Englishman in this matter. I am Irish."[22]

Though the leaders of the British government were reluctant to conscript Irish men for military service, certain forces acting upon them made it necessary. After the German offensive in March, 1918, it was necessary either to conscript Irish men or to raise the age limit for military service from fifty to fifty-five in England, Scotland, and Wales. The British labor unions also were in favor of conscription for Ireland; and, though even Sir Edward Carson thought it was risky, the Ulster Unionists had also been in favor of it. Finally Lloyd George agreed, provided that such conscription was tied to a Home Rule Bill. But it was too late for Home Rule; and, when the Conscription Bill passed the House of Commons, the Irish Nationalist members left the House, returned to Ireland, and joined the Sinn Fein Party in an anti-conscription campaign.[23] Conscription never took effect, but the attempt to impose it led to additional rebellion and to the greater strength of Sinn Fein.

AE had been moving closer and closer to the Sinn Fein position, and Eglinton says that he was only held back from joining the party by two things: his belief that Ireland and Great Britain were economically interdependent and his objection to violence.[24] AE wrote in a letter of January, 1919, to Weekes that "The coming national policy will be a blend of Pearse, Connolly, and AE."[25] This would indeed be a strange blend, and it is difficult to see how the pacifist AE could have accepted the violence of Sinn Fein. There probably was never any possibility of such a fusion, but these expressions on his part reveal how much he was changed by his experience during the Convention.

The Conscription Bill was passed in April. On May 8, 1918, AE wrote a letter to the editor of the *Manchester Guardian*, which appeared later as the pamphlet, *Conscription for Ireland: A Warning to England*.[26] Though he expresses feelings of sympathy for England and his awareness of the feelings of the English people, AE opposes conscription in Ireland on the grounds that Ireland is a separate nation which has never accepted British rule. What the rulers of Britain are trying to overcome is "the soul of a nation":

They have never understood the subjective life of Ireland, because they were contented with domination over all that was apparent. Your people in their schools and universities have been taught that Ireland was an integral part of the United Kingdom. . . . Ireland as a nation disappeared for you, but never so to its own imagination. It never accepted the Union. Never at any time was there a psychic tie corresponding to the physical fact. British authority at all periods in Irish history, as today, rested solely on superior power. There never was a year in the seven centuries of that domination when the vast majority of the people were not opposed to it. When overcome in rebellion they waited sullenly, silently, and steadfastly for the hour of doom falling upon this as upon all empires in history. They desired to manifest their genius in a civilisation of their own. That feeling has been as deep, indeed much deeper, and more selfconscious since the Act of Union was passed; and today, partly through a recovery of the ancient culture, partly by the reaction against State policy, that self-consciousness of nationality is more vivid, passionate, and dominant than at any period in Irish history. (141 - 42)

Basing his argument on the fact of Irish nationality, he warns England to desist in this policy of conscription; and, when he prophesied a rebellion which would last longer than the need for conscription, he was again right. Though conscription never took place, the move to impose it added fuel to the fire of Irish nationalism. As Edgar Holt has put it, "Collins, de Valera and others were setting a slow fuse for an eventual explosion. It was Lloyd George who put the match to it."[27]

During the period of the Anglo-Irish War from 1918 to 1921, AE did not take an active part in the politics or the fighting; but he continued to write letters and pamphlets that commented on the events of the day and that attempted to mold opinion into constructive channels. *A Plea for Justice* is a demand for "a public enquiry into the attacks on co-operative societies in Ireland,"[28] for they had been burned by British forces as reprisals for attacks by the Irish Nationalist irregular forces. The Chief Secretary for Ireland, who had condoned the destruction, had asserted that the cooperatives were centers of revolution. AE, who denies this assertion, appeals to the British people for a fair investigation of the facts: forty-two cooperatives had been burned, with damages estimated at two hundred and fifty to three hundred thousand pounds, and an annual trade loss amounting to about one million pounds.

The occasion of AE's *The Economics of Ireland, and the Policy of the British Government* was the "Better Government of Ireland Bill," which, also known as "the Partition Bill," proposed the division of Ireland into two sections, each with its own parliament. There would be a Joint Council of Ireland, consisting of members nominated by each Parliament, which would bring together representative views on the general affairs of Ireland. The sections then proposed were just as they are today: Northern Ireland, composed of the six northeastern countries (Antrim, Londonderry, Down, Armagh, Tyrone, and Fermanagh); Southern Ireland, the remaining twenty-six counties. Both sections of Ireland would continue to send representatives to Westminster; Great Britain would continue to control the armed forces, foreign relations, the post of-

fice, trade, customs and excise, and other matters of general interest
to both Ireland and the rest of the United Kingdom. This bill might
have been acceptable to Ireland before World War I, except,
possibly, for the partition; but it came too late. The success of Sinn
Fein had given the Irish an idea of what complete freedom would
be like.

In his article, AE opposed two aspects of the bill: English control
over customs and excise, and the partition. He begins with the
assumption that "Whoever controls the taxation and trade policy of
a country controls its destiny and the entire character of its
civilization."[29] Since the new Home Rule Bill still entrusted tax-
ations, trade policy, and the supplying of the armed forces to the
British Parliament, AE believed that wealth would be drained off
and given to Great Britain. He estimated that the annual cost of this
arrangement would be eighteen million pounds, paid as tribute to
Great Britain. This same kind of arrangement existed under the
Ascendency when English landowners used to live in England and
spend in that country the revenue from their holdings in Ireland.
This use of funds was the cause of Irish poverty and of the loss of
population in Ireland.

In his letter, March 25, 1921, to *The Times* AE amplified this loss
to Ireland by the following illustration. The British ministers, said
AE, "can well realize the effect on their own economic system if
Germany had conquered in the late war, had annexed Great Britain
and transferred half the British revenues to Germany to pay for the
building of ships in Germany for its navy, to provide munitions and
clothing for its army."[30] The alternative AE proposed was for the
British to permit Ireland to have control of her own customs and excise, to trade with Britain or any other country of her choice, and to
supply her own portion of the armed forces.

The other portion of the "Partition Bill" which AE opposes is
Lloyd George's "two nation theory," one devised because it was in
the best interest of the Empire to keep Ireland divided:

He [Lloyd George] has painted an imaginative political landscape of
Ireland, a country he has never been in, and expects Ireland to adjust itself
until it becomes like his imaginary political landscape. The Ulsterman and
industrialist is told that the farmers of Ireland will tax him out of existence
if he comes into an all-Irish Parliament. A British finger is pointed at the
Irish Nationalist as the person who will plunder the poor Ulsterman, all the
time another British hand is securely in the Ulster Pocket; and Ulster is being depopulated at exactly the same rate as the other three provinces.[31]

Actually, according to AE, more real wealth is created, contrary to common belief in Southern Ireland than in Northern Ireland. Finally, he asks that Ireland be allowed to develop its own government so that it can realize its destiny as a great civilization; this government would also be free to control its own economic policy, including taxation and trade.

The Inner and the Outer Ireland offers little that is new; but it clearly shows the influence of the Home Rule Convention on AE. The idea of the ancestral self is now seen as Gaelic, and it is only through complete separation from England that this concept may be realized: "The new race made out of the union of Saxon, Dane, Norman, and Gael is still dominated by the last, and it looks back to the Gael as to an ancestral self. The more complex mentality brought about by the commingling of natures is at the service of Ireland and not of its conquerors. The Irish have shown by three hopeless rebellions in every century how loathsome to them is the character in which British statesmen would mold them. I believe that antagonism springs from biological and spiritual necessity."[32]

Obviously, AE had developed greatly as a Nationalist in the seven years between 1914, when he had objected to Plunkett's speech in favor of Home Rule, and 1921 when he expressed this view. He also speaks in this article about the dwindling population of Ireland and its causes: the economic destruction of Ireland by England, the failure of the latest Home Rule Bill to grant Ireland full control of her destiny, and the partition of Ireland.

This article was written just before the Anglo-Irish Treaty and AE was doubtful of a satisfactory settlement. England was too greedy, he believed, to let Ireland have its freedom; and Ireland in its present mood would be satisfied with nothing less. The only hope was for the intervention of a third power, some force from outside to relieve the stalemate. What actually happened was that both sides finally wearied of the fight, and the result was the Treaty; but foreign opinion, chiefly American, probably caused England to weaken in her purpose. AE believed that Ireland would have been satisfied with dominion status at one time, but that this time was now past. In this he was partly right, partly wrong. Some Irishmen, the pro-Treaty party, were willing to accept dominion status; others, the anti-Treaty party, were not; and this difference brought on the Civil War.

The Treaty offered to Ireland was rejected by De Valera but it was ratified by a majority vote of the Dail on January 7, 1922. It gave Ireland dominion status with some minor exceptions, such as

control of naval and air facilities by Great Britain, permission to
recruit for the British forces in Ireland, limitation of the size of the
Irish army, free trade between Ireland and England, and a contribution to Britain's war debt.[33] These differences from the usual
dominion status enjoyed by other dominions were probably dictated
by the proximity to England. Aside from these restrictions, Ireland
was to have complete freedom and autonomy in all governmental
affairs, including economic, legal, military, police, and education
affairs. The main problem was the Oath of Allegiance, and it divided Ireland and brought on the Civil War. De Valera, who never
accepted the oath, eventually caused its abolition.

AE's *Ireland and the Empire at the Court of Conscience*[34] first
appeared on September 22, 1921, in the *Manchester Guardian*
shortly after the offer of the Treaty and before its acceptance on
December 5, 1921. The Treaty was a moment of decision for
Ireland, one that caused much anguish before and after its acceptance. In this article, later published as a pamphlet, AE presented
the arguments on both sides as if a case were being argued before a
court, the "court of conscience." The arguments are too long and
too complex to permit a satisfactory summary, but AE's work
remains an important document for any student who wishes to understand the issues. The arguments for accepting the Treaty indicate the benefits which would be Ireland's if she remained within
the Commonwealth, discuss the insistent minority in Ulster who
refuse to accept independence, and point out the dangers which
may follow if England uses all of her strength to subdue the
rebellion. The arguments against the Treaty are based chiefly on
the assertion that Ireland's destiny is to be free and to express her
genius according to her ancestral tendencies.

AE was able to argue both sides with skill; and, when he defended the Nationalist point of view, he became passionate: "Pearse and
his companions sounded the last trumpet for the Gael, and the dead
were raised up from the graves of fear, unbelief or despair, and out
of a deep sense of identity of being or destiny they reeled after the
shepherds who called. So came Israel out of Egypt" (9). Defining
the situation clearly, AE says that a spiritual level that is above the
claims of reason must be satisfied; and, for the Irish Nationalist, no
reasonable argument can satisfy this claim. AE's presentation is, of
course, inconclusive; but the Nationalist does have the last word.
Nonetheless, AE concludes by saying that it would be better to keep

the struggle on the intellectual and spiritual level than to have it descend to the physical level; for the makings of a modern tragedy are at hand if the right decisions are not made.

III   *The Treaty and the Civil War*

On January 16, 1922, Dublin Castle, long the symbol of British government in Ireland, was turned over to the new Irish Free State. On February 21, AE read to the Sociological Society his paper *Ireland, Past and Future*[35] which is quite general in its scope; for it presents a broad view of the events leading to the Treaty and some predictions for the future. He once again develops his theory of Irish nationality as a manifestation of the Gaelic ancestral self—a theory derived from his old concept of the hero in man, but with a new nationalism grafted onto this metaphysical root. He outlines the differences between Ireland and England and makes a plea for the right of self-determination. AE briefly traces the emergence of the new nationalism that began with the Act of Union and led to Easter Week, and he then summarizes recent developments that include the Anglo-Irish War and the Treaty. His general tone is optimistic; he feels that Ireland is the natural ally of England in spite of recent events and that, once Ireland is free, this natural friendship will flourish.

AE then asks "What about the future?" and attempts some predictions. The four great movements in recent Irish history have been the cooperative movement, the Gaelic Revival, the labor movement, and Sinn Fein. Each of these movements has had its leader, a man of great stature—Sir Horace Plunkett, Douglas Hyde, James Connolly, and Arthur Griffith—but AE is sure that the movements will outlast their leaders. The cooperative movement in agriculture is a necessity, Gaelic will be taught in the schools, and the next generation will be bilingual. The future of Irish labor is more difficult to forecast, but AE feels that some kind of guilds or cooperative productive associations will develop, similar to those suggested in *The National Being*. In politics, he identifies with the pro-Treaty party; but he believes that complete freedom would have been better for Ireland than the dominion status conferred by the Treaty. AE fears that, as long as Ireland is divided, some Nationalists will spend their energy working for the reunification of the country and neglect education and social reform. However, at this point he believes that conflict over the Treaty was not inevitable and that, if a large majority were to vote for the Treaty, its will would be respected. This prediction proved to be wrong.

The intensity of feeling in Northern Ireland against the partition AE attributes chiefly to the inclusion of predominantly Nationalist counties in the partitioned six counties of Northern Ireland. Two logical courses were open in the partition: the first, to include all of historic Ulster, was rejected because the entire province might have voted to join the Free State. The second course, to hold a plebiscite, was also rejected because four counties at most would have voted to separate from the Free State. As a result, two predominantly agricultural counties—Tyrone and Fermanagh—were brought in to balance the labor interests of the four other counties. AE rightly predicted that there would be trouble if these two counties were coerced into union with Northern Ireland, but the trouble in recent times has developed elsewhere and for different reasons.[36]

Though AE was hopeful of a peaceful settlement, he was aware of the savage forces which were ready to tear Ireland apart: "In the shadows in Ireland, North and South, lurks reptilian human life, bigots who in the name of Christ spit upon his precepts and who have put on the whole armoury of hate, and men, and women too, who have known the dark intoxication of blood, and who seek half unconsciously for the renewal of that sinister ecstasy."[37] In spite of AE's hope that the conflict would be settled peacefully, the Civil War began a few days after the prohibited convention of the Irish Republican Army was held at the Mansion House on March 26, 1922; and it ended May 24, 1923, when the final cease-fire was proclaimed by De Valera.

AE, who was by now reckoned as a leader of Irish opinion, was always ready to enter the arena to remonstrate with the extremists. Such a remonstrance was contained in an "Open Letter to Irish Republicans," which appeared in the *Irish Times* on December 29, 1922. In it, AE asks the anti-Treaty party to give up the battle and to work peacefully for the accomplishment of their goals.[38] He agrees with them in their claim about "the natural right of our people to complete independence." But he disagrees with their methods: he is particularly opposed to the use of violence against other Irishmen in a civil war. It is doubtful if many of the Die-Hards understood AE's beautiful and lofty words when he said:

I do not ask you to give up any ideal. I think, if your cause alone is to be considered, a non-military Republicanism would win you more adherents.

Your ideas would take deeper root in men's minds because they would be well-considered, accepted because of their superior beauty or fitness for Irish needs. Adherence to them would not be passional only, arising out of the antagonism between races. I ask you to take as companion to that principle of liberty which you champion the principle of brotherhood; for they are nothing apart from each other, and it is because of their severance that lamentable cry has gone over the world about liberty and the things that are done in its name. The wisdom of hell is to divide and conquer the divine principles, and its religion is to uphold one half of heavenly law so that by that lure good men may fall into the pit.[39]

Although it is difficult to know how much force his words had, they continued to set a sober and decent tone for Irish life; and this attitude was AE's great contribution. He served as the norm of sanity in a time of insanity; and, while he spoke, the world knew that there were decent and wise men in Ireland. After the Civil War, when the new Irish Senate was established, AE was invited to become a senator, but he refused the honor.[40] This response was typical of him.

In January, 1929, AE wrote in retrospect the article "Twenty-five Years of Irish Nationality"[41] for *Foreign Affairs;* and in it, he recapitulates the history of the Anglo-Irish War and the Civil War, as well as the origins of modern Irish nationalism. He emphasizes the Gaelic Revival; the work of Standish O'Grady in literature; the Irish Literary Revival and the work of Yeats, Lady Gregory, and Synge; Sinn Fein, James Connolly, and the labor movement; and the Irish Volunteers. In this article, we learn some of the events that were going on behind the scenes, such as how Constance Markiewicz acted as the go-between for Pearse and Connolly and brought together the forces of revolution and labor. The true meaning of the Easter Week Rising and its influence on the development of Irish nationalism is clarified in this passage: "These men had died for their country. None could laugh at them anymore. They had spoken greatly, but life cannot utter greater words than it can meet by sacrifice. High talk with them was equalled by high fate. The price was paid, and all over Ireland young men who had thought but lightly of the leaders of that revolution while living, recoiled from their cynicism and brooded on the heroes and martyrs of their country in pride and penitence."[42]

AE tells us here that the sacrifices of these men touched him personally: they changed him and made him more nationalistic. However, he never gave up his ideal of cooperation nor his hatred of violence. We realize the extent of AE's contribution to Irish independence when he tells us here that Lord Northcliffe, proprietor of the London *Times*, asked what he could do to help; and AE convinced him that his paper could help by bringing American opinion to bear on the English consciousness. He believed that Ireland would never have reached its goal of freedom without the pressure of this opinion.

In the concluding paragraphs, AE deals with Ireland of 1929—its progress, its hopes, its fears. AE felt that, culturally and economically, things were going well and that the leaders of the government were able and honest. The country had been reorganized, taxes had been lowered, and the country was peaceful. A new unarmed police force had been created, and a Civil Service Commission had eliminated jobbery and patronage. The great weakness of the country, he felt, was in education. Since eighty percent of the people had left school by the age of twelve, they had hardly emerged from the folk state of mind; and they were therefore unable to make wise decisions about political issues. But he felt that this situation was improving and that the country was becoming more aware of the external world and of its own relationship to the world community. His hope was that Ireland would retain its national identity but that, at the same time, it would become more aware of its external relationships and obligations.

AE was a statesman in the finest sense, because he placed the welfare of the nation above his own welfare and ambition. He was not a politician, and his experience with the Home Rule Convention indicates that he had no patience with those who were. During the period covered in this chapter, from 1913 to 1923, he became more nationalistic by believing in the necessity of complete independence for all of Ireland but one with a more productive and mutually beneficial relationship with the United Kingdom. Though he hated violence, he realized that it was necessary in the Anglo-Irish War to make English leaders aware of the dedication and resolution of Irish nationalism. In the Civil War, AE's hatred of violence was even greater, because it had involved fratricide and the destruction of national ideals. He believed in the duty of citizens to speak against unwise, illegal, and inhuman actions; and he did not fear to express his views clearly and forcefully. It is probably in the sphere of political and economic theory and action that he reveals the greatest development; and, if he had had the same kind of stimulus in the artistic area that he found in the political sphere, he probably would have shown greater development there. Some of his most compelling prose belongs to this period when the exciting events of the day challenged his greatness and made him speak out with sincerity and force.

CHAPTER 7

AE as Critic: The Last Years

IN the spring of 1923, the anti-Treaty forces surrendered in their struggle for a free and united Ireland. In September of the same year, *The Irish Homestead* merged with *The Irish Statesman*; and AE spent most of the remaining years of his life as editor of this interesting and unusual Irish journal. AE did much of the writing himself under various pennames: "AE," "Y.O.," "O.L.S.," and "Gab," to name a few. The purpose of this anonymous writing was chiefly to save money, and the result was a kind of unity which stamped the paper with the personality of AE. Eglinton describes his writing in *The Irish Statesman* as "vigorous thought" and as "noble writing." Eglinton continues, "In a single number we find (all written by himself) well-informed notes on current topics, home and foreign; at least one brilliant leading article; a literary or philosophical 'causerie'; a poem; book reviews; besides that part of the paper which continued the work of the *Irish Homestead.*"[1]

After AE became editor of *The Irish Homestead* in August,1905, he remained at that post through all of the bitter struggles for independence; but he also delivered speeches and wrote books. His genius as an editor improved that paper; for, as Eglinton has declared, " . . . AE's journalism rose like a song out of the bitter newspaper press of Ireland. . . . People who looked into the *Irish Homestead* to see how AE would write about pigs and poultry shrugged their shoulders when they found perfectly readable discourses, with glints of science, metaphysics and the lore of the East, and hints of AE's peculiar doctrines. . . ."[2]

The Irish Statesman gave AE greater freedom and scope than *The Irish Homestead* had; for, no longer restricted to Ireland and agriculture, he was able to develop international and literary themes in the paper. He could write on poetry, painting, economics, philosophy, religion, and all the varied subjects that interested him.

The titles given to selections in Monk Gibbon's *The Living Torch*, an anthology of AE's writings for *The Irish Statesman*, show the tremendous range of AE's interests: "Censorship," "Imagination and the Ideal State," "Whitehead and Religion," "Reason and Intuition," "Religion and Science," "Women and Civilization," "Boxers," "The Eternal Feminine," "The Dublin Record Office," "Drunkenness," "Emigration," "The Nation and Beauty," "Peace," "Suffering," "Endurance," and "Foolishness" are a few of them.

The Irish Statesman did not adhere to any party line; and this fact, according to Eglinton, limited its influence and effectiveness. Being in the center of the spectrum of opinion, the paper was attacked from both sides: " . . . The anti-Treaty group were outraged that the paper upheld the Anglo-Irish settlement, and the pro-Treaty group denounced its half-heartedness in dealing with the Republican extremists. The North objected to its appeal for Irish unity as strenuously as the South did [to] its recognition that the political partition was an established fact."[3]

The editorial position of *The Irish Statesman* was that Ireland must be unified, both the Irish and the pro-English elements. Furthermore, a purely Gaelic state was unrealizable, for Ireland could not rely on its own resources. Ireland must be finally unified, with friendly relations to Great Britain.[4] The chief strength of *The Irish Statesman* was its attention to literature and to literary criticism, and it effected a new literary revival similar to the earlier one which had centered around the Abbey Theatre and W. B. Yeats in the years between 1900 and 1910. AE in his paper brought to the fore new names in literature: Oliver St. John Gogarty, Monk Gibbon, Austin Clarke, Hugh MacDiarmid, Patrick Kavanagh, F. R. Higgins, Frank O'Connor, Sean O'Casey, and Liam O'Flaherty—names that have since become well known in Irish literature.

AE's deputy editor was James Winder Good, who died in 1930. Susan L. Mitchell was AE's editorial assistant until her death in 1926. She was a great help to AE and served as a kind of maid-of-all-work after the merger of the *Homestead* with the *Statesman*. After Miss Mitchell's death, AE's younger son, Diarmuid Russell, joined the staff and wrote book reviews as Miss Mitchell had done before him. Even with all of this able help, the paper took most of AE's time. in his letter of August 2, 1925, to Ernest A. Boyd, he says: "I find the *Statesman* a horrible grind, have no leisure for anything else, and it is not much pleasure writing it as the country is insensitive in the re-action against all the excitement."[5] Nevertheless, he continued as editor until the paper ceased publication on April 12, 1930.

An anthology of AE's prose writings was published in 1937 by Monk Gibbon under the title *The Living Torch*. Since this book is readily available in libraries, more available than the files of the *Statesman*, Dr. Gibbon's book is the basis of this account of AE's last years as an editor and critic. Of his selection, Dr. Gibbon writes: "Practically everything in this present book has been drawn from *The Irish Statesman*, and in reading it we will do well to remember its period—post-war Europe and post-treaty Ireland—and also the circumstances under which it was produced, in haste, with little revision and often while the printer's devil waited. We must not judge it in the same way that we would judge his finished work."[6] Although Gibbon also admits that it was necessary to rearrange much of AE's material, to give titles to it, and to divide it into sections, anyone who has read AE's work recognizes that AE is really speaking to us in these pages.

AE expresses his ideas about the following topics: (1) the nature of literature and poetry, (2) the criticisms of various poets, (3) painting and the visual arts, (4) philosophy and psychology, (5) history, (6) the nation and political questions, (7) America and the United States. Between 1928 and 1935, AE visited the United States four times; he travelled widely across the continent and developed some rather radical and penetrating ideas about it that may still be instructive to us today. Since his ideas in these pages are the mature thought of his long life, they seem to be a fitting way to conclude this introduction to his life and work.[7]

I   *The Nature of Literature and Poetry*

For AE, literature was as much a form of religion as it was for the Romantic and Transcendental writers from whom his theory developed. In a description of the Enneads of Plotinus, he compares the act of translation with original composition. Where the translator works deliberately, the creator works under the guidance of imagination. We do not consciously select our words in creation; we write or speak as they are given to us by an internal spiritual source. "The imagination of man," he says, "is a despotic genie and words are its trembling slaves who wait obediently on it to mirror its

lightest motions" (108). In an article about Tolstoi, AE writes that
". . . the artist sings, paints or writes out of a spiritual necessity,
and in the blindness of creation he is not thinking of other people at
all. In the conflagration set up he illuminates his own being, the self
is made clear to the self, and there is a profounder self-
consciousness after creation. It may happen that the lamp he lights
may give light to others, but we are certain that nothing first-class
came when the artist's mind was fixed on his public rather than on
his subject" (307 - 08). The writer writes only for the purpose of
truth or self-expression and not from any ulterior motive. Echoing a
statement from Keat's letters, AE says "The making of poetry
should be as natural with us as the blossoming of the hedgerows
. . . " (85). Also, the poet should write with his whole being, not
just a part of himself.

AE's standard for poetry and literary ideas was essentially a
Platonic one that was derived from the *Symposium* where, according to AE, Plato had established a hierarchy of ideas. The first of
this hierarchy is love of a single person or form; this quality ascends
to awareness of beauty in other forms, then to an awareness of the
beauty of ideas; and it culminates in an awareness of essential beauty. From this Platonic ladder, AE develops a distinction between
opaque and transparent poetry. Opaque poetry is superficial and
gives us only appearances, but transparent poetry gives us a view
into the essential nature of things. We are imprisoned by the
opaque ideas, but liberated by the transparent (105). Opaque ideas
are not bad, merely limited: We are satisfied by their loveliness, but
we are not permitted to transcend them. Transparent ideas, on the
other hand, open new vistas for us and lead to the spiritual aspect of
life, to imagination, to beauty, and to truth. For this reason, AE
preferred the Symbolist movement to the Imagist movement; for
the Symbolists lead us to spirit, while the Imagists provide only new
views of the earth.

Poetry is the highest form of literature, and its purpose is an ascent to the spirit world. Since poetry and prose have their own distinct purposes, poetry should not be used for the purposes of prose.
Poetry should be spiritual; prose, intellectual (300 - 02). Examples
of the misuse of poetry are provided by Robert Browning and
Robert Graves. In his article captioned "The Hen in Eagle's
Feathers" (297 - 300), he describes how Browning in "Sludge the
Medium," "Bishop Bloughram's Apology," and some of his other
dramatic monologues uses poetic expression where prose would

have been more fitting. Robert Graves commits the same fault when he puts an imaginary letter from one soldier to another in verse. Free verse might be the appropriate form for such borderline modes of expression; but, "To write poetry, whether one uses traditional metrics or free-verse forms, is to essay the highest spiritual adventures, and every word should be weighed as if the space it occupies was more valuable than diamonds, and not a line be allowed to pass that is not like a living thing shapely enough to keep companionship with the creatures of melody created by the great masters" (236). A poet who has not succeeded in writing such poetry is Eva Gore-Booth, friend of W. B. Yeats and sister of the famous Countess Markievicz. AE feels that she wrote too hurriedly and did not take sufficient care to write only the best. She thought she would lose the mood if she did not write her poems immediately, and she failed to realize that poetry is first imagined in the "dream consciousness" and is then brought to realization in the "waking consciousness." Both of these consciousnesses are subject to a censor, the "aesthetic conscience," which will not permit poetry to pass until its idea and form are in harmony.

AE seemed to feel that rhythm was important in poetry but that prosody as then understood was inadequate as a guide to the appropriate rhythms of poetry. Prosody and scansion are too mechanical; a sense of rhythm and rhyme should come naturally; and a strict examination of metrics was of little value if it did *not* come naturally. AE cites the example of an unnamed poet who knew nothing of the science of prosody but whose poetry was rhythmical. He feels that it might be possible to discover something about the nature of verbal music in poetry by "taking some fifty or hundred of the loveliest verses in the language and subjecting them to minute analysis so that assonance, contrast of vowel and consonant, pattern, tone, stress, all that goes to make a quality of sound might be made clear as far as possible" (236 - 37). He rightly realizes that simple scansion which employs only a counting of stressed syllables is not adequate for an analysis of the sounds of poetry. Modern linguistic science with its techniques of analysis which describe stress, pitch, and junctures (pauses), is now capable of making such a study, but only a few efforts have been made in this direction.

The ultimate question we must ask about any poet is "From how deep a life does he speak?" Ultimately, the personality, the genius, the sincerity, the soul of the poet determine the quality of his poetry

(100): "The artist asks of a work of art whether it gives us itself only or whether it multiplies images of beauty in us to whom it is given; or, to put it another way, he has genius who can make us see the beauty he sees, but he is a master who can give us his own power of seeing" (125). For AE, the final aim of all true art, including poetry and painting, is to enable us to attain seership or the ability to behold the divine. The final purpose of all art is religious.

One of the chief questions in Ireland at this time was concerned with the language of poetry—What language should a poet use for poetry, English or Irish? Many Nationalist writers felt that Irish was the only language for an Irish poet. In "A Gaelic Literature," AE answers this question. First, a writer should write in the language which will permit him to reach the greatest number of readers, all other things being equal. Second, he should write in the language which permits him to express himself best: If this is Irish, then he should write in Irish. However, AE questions whether Irish, an ancient language, has evolved sufficiently to reflect the subtleties of the modern mind and the modern world. Third, he admits that the knowledge of Irish permits a person to read and use the ancient Gaelic literature, "the great almost untapped reservoir in Europe of primitive natural imagination and beauty." Since AE realizes that he is treading on dangerous ground, as this question was a vital Nationalist one at that time, he states that he is not opposed to Gaelic; he merely questions its purpose and use (238 - 40).

II *Criticisms of Various Poets*

AE discusses many writers in the articles collected in *The Living Torch*, beginning with Shakespeare and coming up to modern times with James Joyce, Gertrude Stein, and James Stephens. As we might expect, he liked the Romantic poets, William Blake, William Wordsworth, Percy Bysshe Shelley, and John Keats, and their American cousins, Ralph Waldo Emerson, Henry David Thoreau, and Walt Whitman. He did not particularly care for the moderns, such as T. S. Eliot, James Joyce, and Ezra Pound, because he felt that they did not write from the depths but from the surface of life. In a letter written to Frank O'Connor in January, 1934, he said that "The poets like Eliot and Spender have no light in their minds. They are the dead end, and when Eliot writes a volume of criticism of poetry the effect is to make me never want to read poetry any more in the world, the criticism is so dry and joyless."[8]

AE believed that the modern tendency which he thought to be heading into a blind alley had begun with Shakespeare. While he acknowledged Shakespeare's greatness in mastery of the language, he also felt that he was pivotal in the history of literature. Literature before Shakespeare depicted man under the influence of spiritual powers: "The greatest of Greek dramas leaves us with this sense that the characters meet to reveal something greater than themselves." But Shakespeare was concerned with character for its own sake, and he was probably the first great author to be so concerned (111 - 14).

AE had great admiration for John Keats, and his writing shows a familiarity with the letters of Keats. He agreed with Keats that poetry must grow organically and naturally from within the poet, he believed that Keats's own poetry grew in this way, and he thought that Keats was second only to Shakespeare in his mastery of language (115 - 16). Blake was another of AE's favorites, as we might expect, because he combined poetry, vision, and pictorial art. There is more of the element of infinity in Blake than in any of his contemporaries, according to AE, and thus he is less easily exhausted. Blake excites us, even when we do not entirely understand him. "His mind has not yet been completely charted," says AE; and he quotes Emerson as saying that we can bridge the distance between body and First Cause by the use of the mind: "That is, we seem to run up and down a ladder set in clay, which at its highest touches divinity. Most of us are on the lower rungs, but Blake seems to ascend and descend with a swiftness which was bewildering to those who spoke to him, and which I suspect, was sometimes bewildering to himself" (117).

AE does not think Blake was mad. His apparent insanity was the result of his inability to explain his visions to his contemporaries. His visions came from his active imagination and most people could not understand them. Of "Blake's Prophetic Books," AE says that Blake was a pioneer in the world of the spirit, where he discovered new and strange creatures. He gave them names because they had no names before he discovered them: "All these creatures are but parts of our own nature dramatically sundered from the primordial unity of the spirit" (118 - 21).

AE's favorite American poet is Walt Whitman, though Emerson and Thoreau follow him closely. These three are Transcendentalists, unlike those writers who followed them—William James, Henry Adams, George Santayana, John Dewey, William Dean Howells, Upton Sinclair, Jack London, Theodore Dreiser, Sinclair Lewis,

Sherwood Anderson, Carl Sandburg, Vachel Lindsay, Robert Frost, and Edwin Arlington Robinson. To AE, these writers are "all men of some force and talent but no sky-touching genius, no one even who burrows as deeply as our James Joyce" (321). Of Thoreau, AE says that he was capable of approaching nature directly without the aid of books, libararies, theaters, or other artificial stimuli. Thoreau's mind "seemed to catch fire from Nature itself" (328).

What put Whitman above Thoreau and Emerson is not made entirely clear by AE; perhaps it was his originality of expression, his ability to express his ideas in a new medium appropriate to his thought. He was the first important poet to attempt free verse and to commit his poetry to it almost exclusively. Sometimes it degenerates into prose: "He would cry out, 'Land of beef! Land of pork! Land of cotton!' in an ecstasy incomprehensible to any, except perhaps a dealer in those commodities who had made a profitable contract" (234). Sometimes Whitman fails, but more often he succeeds beautifully, as in "When Lilacs Last in the Dooryard Bloomed," where he successfully develops a free organic verse admirably suited to the thought.

But more important is the reader's feeling that Whitman, unlike Tolstoi, loves mankind; and AE's comparison between Tolstoi and Whitman rests on this difference. While AE admitted the genius, intelligence, and abnormal power of concentration which Tolstoi possessed, he disliked his moralizing. Tolstoi was a great novelist, possibly the greatest; but he was a preacher who rejected beauty because he could not define it. We might as well reject God because of the conflicting views of His nature. But with Whitman, art is a mode of being, not a vehicle for morality. AE quotes Whitman as saying that " 'The oration is to the orator, and comes most back to him. The poem is to the poet, and comes most back to him. The painting is to the painter, and comes most back to him.' That is, the artist sings, paints, or writes out of a spiritual necessity, and in the blindness of creation he is not thinking of other people at all. . . . We can agree with Tolstoi that the greatest art is religious, and when the spiritual element is lacking the art is inferior in substance. But I doubt the spirituality of Tolstoi even when he talks most about religion" (307 - 08). As we might expect, AE's distinction is between religion and spirituality: a poet can write about religion and yet not attain to the spiritual. Whitman is a seer, a man with a vision of the divine; but Tolstoi merely talks about religion and morality.

The Irish writers in whom AE seemed most interested were Yeats,

Joyce, Shaw, Synge, O'Casey, and Stephens. He respected Yeats chiefly for his ideal of perfection, which he felt was unsurpassed by any poet then writing in English. Yeats had made the name and the landscape of Ireland important and familiar to the rest of the world, more so than had the political figures who had come to fame during the Anglo-Irish War. AE also respected him for his vision and imagination, but he preferred his earlier to his later style, for AE felt that Yeats had become more self-conscious as he grew older and therefore less attuned to the spiritual (263 - 64). Still, he admired Yeats's later style as he makes clear in his review of *The Winding Stair* when he says that he has been trying to understand the development of Yeats's style with its "new and strange beauty." AE admits the stylistic development and the greater intellectuality of the later verse: "It is one of the rarest things in literature to find a poet of whom it might be said that his wine was like that in the feast in the Scriptures, where the best was kept until the last." Yeats's "intellectual adventures into philosophy, mysticism and symbolism, into magic and spiritualism" and his development of unusual modes of thought were responsible for this stylistic and intellectual advance (91 - 94).

AE agreed with Yeats that "we make poetry out of the quarrel with ourselves," but he was distrustful of *A Vision*, Yeat's baffling explanation of his mystical system. In this book, Yeats had developed what he called a "lunar parable," explaining the various phases of history in terms of the revolution of the moon around the earth. Periods of history like the Renaissance were subjective and related to the full moon, while periods like our modern scientific era are objective and related to the dark of the moon. People are also governed by the phases of the moon, an engineer or mathematician being objective, an artist or poet being subjective. The lunar phase a person was assigned to under this system was, therefore, related to his personality and his achievements. The system, obviously, was a fusion of astrology, history, and psychology. There is some question whether Yeats was serious about it as an explanation of history; he merely said it gave him metaphors for his poetry.

In an article about Yeats's *Per Amica Silentia Lunae*, the antecedent of *A Vision*, AE writes: "When we have explained ourselves to ourselves too clearly the quarrel is settled. I would rather the poet fished in that rich darkness for creatures of the mind which blaze when they are brought into full consciousness" (91). He also objected to *A Vision* and its system because of its determinism, questioning the complexity and arbitrary nature of the system. For example, he was surprised to find himself grouped in the same lunar phase with Calvin, Luther, and Newman; but he was pleased to find himself classed with George Herbert, the English religious poet. AE wondered if Yeats were joking, but he should have known Yeats better than that after all the years they had been acquainted. The system is coherent, AE thought, but he questioned its relationship to life. *A Vision* is not a book that will be read in our time, he said, but in future years it may be compared with the books of Blake. Though AE had his reservations, he was glad that Yeats had written the book; but he would like to have rewritten it and to have left out the cyclic theory (252 - 56). His objection to the system is based on the fact that it limits free will, an element essential to AE's philosophy. We wonder, however, what would have been left if the cyclic system had been removed from *A Vision* since it is so important not only to the book itself but also to so many of Yeats's poems.

Joyce, AE believed, had a great but misdirected talent which lay chiefly in his language. AE's criticism centers around two main objects: his language and the area of human life which he treats. Joyce's language is vital and exciting, and he has done for literature what the post-Impressionists, Cubists, and Futurists have done for modern painting: He had freed it from academic tradition and made it more personal and spontaneous. Although Joyce has enriched modern literature, he would have done even more for it had he explored the heights of consciousness instead of digging into the depths (333 - 34). "I wish," says AE, "he had tried to penetrate into the palace chambers rather than into the crypts and cellars and sewers of the soul, and written after *Ulysses* the effort of his hero to rise out of that Inferno through a Purgatorio to a Paradiso" (140). This wish reveals not only AE's spiritual bias but his failure to understand the nature of modern literature. As Yeats might have said, AE was out of phase with the world spirit: he was a spiritual and religious man in a materialistic and anti-religious era.

AE preferred Stephens to Synge and O'Casey because Stephens writes of the heroic past while the other two describe the purely human condition of Ireland's present. Although these authors contribute to the national imagination and to the national being, AE is afraid to speculate about what will come out of the lawlessness of *The Playboy of the Western World*. But he is not afraid to speculate about O'Casey, and he hopes that the pity O'Casey has inspired will affect the national life for the better, possibly even contributing to the destruction of the slums which are a blight on Irish life (136).

AE admired Shaw, the last saint of Ireland and "the ascetic prophet of our generation," for his wit and his sense of justice. Since Shaw's mission, according to AE, was "to quicken or vitalize the torpid mental body of humanity by shooting into it the electrifying shafts of his wit" (171) he transformed the drama from an amusement to an intellectual exercise. His sense of justice was the second thing that AE noticed; for although almost irrefutable, Shaw's sense of justice has only three dimensions,—but AE has a fourth dimension. AE's additional dimension is a sense of eternal and divine justice that is expressed by the Indian religion as Karma and by Christianity as the idea that as a man sows, so shall he reap. AE feels that since Shaw misses this spiritual element, he is therefore earthbound (332 - 33).

III *Painting and the Visual Arts*

Painting was AE's favorite avocation, and his writing for *The Irish Statesman* reflects this interest. His articles on art include pieces about artists as far apart as Leonardo da Vinci, William Blake, Dante Gabriel Rossetti, Vincent Van Gogh, Jack Yeats, Gustave Moreau, Michaelangelo, and Harry Clark. As in his literary criticism, AE believed that inward vision was most important in great art; that, if the artist lacked this spiritual vision, his painting would be unimportant. Good workmanship is also important, but is not sufficient for lasting art. The museums are full of paintings which are uninspired, ones which follow the conventions but do nothing more. Leonardo and Blake are artists of vision, but this important quality is lacking in Rossetti, Moreau, and Burne-Jones. Leonardo's works depict the mixture of his "waking consciousness" and his "dream consciousness;" body and spirit coexist in perfect harmony; neither achieves mastery over the other:

Take some of those wonderful heads. You will find in one, while the eyes are melting the lips are cold; in another, the eyes are scornful while the lips allure. How are we to interpret this? Is it not the art of one who has seen into two worlds, who saw the beauty of body and of spirit, and who tried to unite incompatibles which cannot live equally together because one must be the slave of the other? In these strange, beautiful faces spirit is never the master of flesh, nor has the body made the spirit its slave. They coexist, superimposed on each other, by the magic of his art, beauties which war upon each other in life. It is the marrriage of Heaven and Hell, which so many artists and poets have tried to paint. (275)

This same quality attracts AE to Blake, the poet and painter who more than any other artist attempted in his poems and pictures to unite Heaven and Hell.

In an article about Blake's symbolic designs, AE questions the origin of Blake's images and thinks that a psychological study of Blake would be more productive than interpretations. AE wonders if the designs of Blake originate in his "waking consciousness" as the result of his apprehension of physical forms or if they originate in the inner vision of the artist as symbolic representations of ideas given to him by some transcendental power. This question AE would have asked of psychology, but he would probably have been doomed to disappointment because psychology does not answer such questions. His own conclusion is that Blake's figures may be of two different kinds: those which have some "external psychic reality," and those which are the result of internal vision. But AE is forced to deny any external reality to most of these figures (121 - 22).

Though AE shared with Rossetti the idea that art is an end in itself, his general impression of Rossetti's work was low. Some of his early work had intensity of imagination, but, generally, he lacked vision. His painting of "The Blessed Damozel" is "sinister and vulgar," AE feels that Rossetti may have depended too much on drugs to heighten his psychic intensity, and his impression of this art work is that the "blessed damozel" is " . . . A clammy, vampirish creature, while behind her in Paradise a score of behaloed lovers are hugging and kissing each other passionately. Rossetti's conception of Paradise seems to have been a sublimated Hampstead Heath on holiday, with ' 'Arry' and ' 'Arriet' in erotic abandonment" (276). To AE, Van Gogh is perhaps superior to Rossetti as a painter, but he doubts that the intensity in his work is truly spiritual or the result of vision; the intensity results more from "that exasperation of the nerves which finally developed into madness" (271 - 72).

AE's art criticism is clear, incisive, and well-formed by his own experience as a painter. He seems to feel secure in his judgments, which rest on his solid conviction that all art must be the product of

inner vision and that the greater the spirit of the artist, the greater
his art will be.

IV *Philosophy and Psychology*

Another group of articles in *The Irish Statesman* covered a range
of topics which may best be considered as the criticism of ideas.
Since AE was well read in both ancient and modern authors, his articles covered thinkers as widely different as Plotinus, Jacob
Boehme, Carl G. Jung, Sigmund Freud, Alfred Adler, and Sir
Jagadis Chandra Bose; but he quite naturally preferred those
thinkers who agreed with his concepts of the spiritual nature of the
universe. Although AE was a firm believer in the transcendence of
mind and spirit over matter, he could not be called a dualist
because he accepted the world of matter: He felt that it was alive
and that it had to be perceived spiritually. His reading of the Indian
scientist, Sir Jagadis Bose, bore out his belief that matter has life of
its own. Bose, he said, "has demonstrated the existence of a
pulsating heart in trees and plants following upon his discovery of
the possession by plants of a muscular tissue." The same author had
earlier found "a life current in metals" which could be killed,
brought to life, and affected by narcotics (204).

AE objected to Darwinian theory because it insists on the struggle
for existence, which is contrary to his own belief in the essential harmony of the universe and the necessity of cooperation. He looked
for a scientist who would show the life and spirit of the universe.
Everything we have read of AE's lifelong struggle for a cooperative
way of life leads us to believe that Darwin would not be one of his
favorite thinkers; and, in fact, AE believed that Darwin's theory was
now "almost obsolete." AE clearly felt that the modern anti-
spiritual tendency was merely a phase of the world-soul's journey
through time, and that it would someday be replaced by a more
spiritual world-view.

Modern thinkers, such as William James, Henri Bergson,
Benedetto Croce, and Herbert Spencer, also reflect this anti-
spiritual tendency; and they are far inferior, therefore, to such great
masters of the spirit as Plotinus. Modern psychology and psychiatry
in particular AE felt to be so governed by materialistic doctrines
that he had to go as far back as Jacob Boehme (1575 - 1624) before
he found any real spiritual thinkers (286 - 89). Psychologists like
Freud, Jung, and Adler are not men of wide culture in AE's estima-

tion because they had depended on a narrow scientific education to generate their theories of the soul. These men seize upon an idea or a mood, and from that they generate a whole system of philosophy.

Of Adler, he writes that "We get the impression from Adler of a clever little soul having become self-conscious of a mood in itself, making this mood fundamental in life. We can imagine a whole succession of psychologists, each obsessed by a single mood, it may be an erotic mood, or the sense of inferiority, or fear, or ambition, or some other mood, but out of this the psychologist will build a philosophy, and there will be enough people obsessed by the same mood to give him thousands of adherents" (293). What AE objects to here is the generalization of a whole system from a single idea or mood, instead of the development of a system in which the spirit is central. Although he disposes of Jung in much the same fashion, AE really did not have sufficient knowledge of psychology or of psychiatry to entitle him to such wide-sweeping judgments.

What he mainly objected to in Freud and Jung was the idea that repression is bad for the soul, for AE believed that asceticism was good for the soul. In an article about suffering, he says that, "To be able to deny the clamour of emotions and desires, the apparitions of Nature, the appetites of the body, to compel them to be silent, or remote, to experience this power is to experience soul, an entity, self-moving, acting by its own inherent vitality" (207). This view contrasts with the following passage by Jung: "When the Ascetic has succeeded in repressing the evil side of his nature, he may be assured that it is flourishing below the threshold—all the more dangerous because no longer faced consciously" (291).

AE questions whether this view of Jung's is true, for the idea that an evil impulse resisted still lives in the subconscious suggests to AE a mechanistic view of the psyche which he cannot accept. Man must be capable of controlling his own ego, or he is a mere machine under the control of a power which has no purpose or goal. AE also objects to Jung's concept of the collective unconscious even though it appears at first glance to be similar to his own concept of *anima mundi*.[9] The difference is that Jung's concept of the collective unconscious is mechanistic and that AE's idea of the *anima mundi* is spiritual. AE, who believes quite correctly that Jung sees the collective unconscious as a hereditary element that resides in the germ cell, suggests that the germ cell is already overworked, and that the idea of acquired characteristics being inherited was exploded long ago by the work of August Weismann (291 - 93).

AE's opposition to such ideas was neither rigid nor doctrinaire; and, for an amateur, he seems to have an excellent grasp of these concepts. He simply wanted to assure that all ideas would be known; for, in another article, he writes of the "one-dimensional mind obsessed by a single idea or passion." Persons with this single dimension lack the flexibility required to accept other ideas and to change their views. They seize on "opaque symbols" such as "the Republic" and refuse to consider other possible alternatives (191 - 93). Since there is no way to determine what the effect of an idea is or will be, the only hope is to have the most free exchange of ideas in a given society (229). All ideas are potentially dangerous, as exemplified by those of Hegel which may have led to the autocratic state that caused a series of wars unparalleled in European history. He does not specify which ideas of Hegel's but he is probably thinking of Marx's adaptation of Hegel's theory to produce dialectical materialism. Although AE does not mention the theories of Karl Marx, these theories (which owe much to Hegel's dialectical system) would probably have been condemned by AE as being materialistic and deterministic. He also cites the development of Sinn Fein as one idea that had far-reaching consequences, and he suggests the importance and dangers that new ideas may have: "We are everywhere surrounded with perils. We cannot do with ideas. Neither can we do without them. The idea, perhaps a dangerous one, occurs to me, that every idea has its antitoxin; the idea which neutralizes its effect; and a college of sages might be founded to examine all new ideas to discover whether they are dangerous" (229).

V   *History and Myth: Nation and Politics*

Another group of AE's articles deals with the writing of history, the nature of myth, and the influence of great men in history. AE believed that historians do not give enough attention to the spiritual causes of historical events. Wars, for example, he saw as the result of "conflicting imaginations" and treaties "are the equilibrium after the imaginative storm has worn itself out." Nations can be defined only in psychic terms, for a nation is "an imagination common to millions of people" (134). Great men like Napoleon are the spiritual forces which shape history, but he may have been a "dark avatar," an instrument of the divine mind used to change history. AE seems to feel that, since there is a balance in nature, the good is balanced by the evil; a Napoleon, by a Jesus.

Power itself has a spiritual explanation, being a kind of radioactive force. He finds something mystical about the mesmeric power of a Napoleon—something inexplicable by any other explanation than a spiritual one (313). Leaders such as Napoleon become heroes of legends and myths, and later heroes then relive the lives of these earlier men. Thus myths are true in that mythical heroes represent national moods; and, whenever the national mood is reawakened, these mythical heroes are reincarnated. Padraic Pearse assumed such a role when he led the Easter Rebellion of 1916, for he had relived the life of Cuchulain. Shakespeare's imaginary Henry V is just as real as Mary of Scotland was. Poets like Burns, Moore, and Yeats help to re-create the national moods, and in this way they influence history by helping to create nations (134 - 35).

In a group of articles about the nation and beauty, the need for a national imagination, and the ugliness of commercialism, AE agrees with the views of John Ruskin and William Morris that the truly healthy nation must have an imagination of its own and a love of beauty and culture; for, to AE, "Let beauty fade, and in some mysterious way public spirit, sacrifice, enthusiasm also vanish from society" (183). A nation cannot exist without a sense of beauty any more than the body can without a soul. The practice that depresses AE more than any other is that of using billboards or hoardings that contain advertisements for commercial products: "Man has a power of creating ugliness which no other animal can approach to. It is the dark or obverse side of his power of creating beauty. Every higher faculty in man has its dark or demoniac side, and the problem is how to prevent people who have lost the feeling for beauty offending sense and soul in those who have it still" (186). Because human nature, like all nature, is two-sided, man is capable of both beauty and ugliness. Ireland needed the development of learning and culture to replace the bitterness of the past. The old Anglo-Irish aristocracy had this culture; but it had not reached the popular level. AE wanted to create a popular culture which would give the people the taste, learning, and culture that would replace the rifle of revolutionary days with books and the arts. Yeats, who had had this desire earlier, had become so disillusioned that he had retreated into his symbolic and aristocratic tower at Ballylee; but AE never lost sight of this goal (193 - 96).

AE had the ability to draw general truths from limited data, as his writings of this period show. Following the First World War and the Irish Troubles, he made statements about Ireland which were true then and are even more so today. AE pointed out the dangers of a

nation that exceeded its income, engaged in a purely military
stance, and neglected domestic problems in order to fight inter-
minable wars. He thought that two paths were possible for the nation which desires to achieve greatness: first, to employ "the higher
human faculties of imagination and intellect." The second, "the
way of physical force for those who prefer to live in the bodily
plane" (220 - 22). Of prolonged wars, AE wrote, "We believe no
cause, however intrinsically noble in itself, but will lead to the
degradation of the finer attributes of humanity if it involves the
people in a prolonged conflict" (221). In an article which commented about Yeats's winning of the Nobel Prize in 1923, AE wrote
that, in order to have a good society, a nation needs a literature
which adds beauty and delight to its people's lives. If men contemplate images of violence, they will become violent; but, if they
contemplate images of beauty, they will live beautiful lives (258).
As AE so often stated, "We become like what we contemplate;" or,
to quote another of his favorite phrases, "As is our aspiration, so is
our inspiration."

Generally, AE's impression of civilization in his later years was
pessimistic. He still talked about the "uncorrupted spiritual atom,"
but he had little hope that it would prevail over the corrupted mass.
He perceived a unity in older civilizations, such as that of ancient
Greece, which was not visible to him in Europe during the last years
of his life. He saw the period since the Middle Ages, as did many
other thinkers, as a loss of faith and the destruction of the unity of
culture. His hope was that Ireland, through a recovery of vision,
might lead the way to a restoration of this unity of culture. This
could only be achieved by "sacrifice, agony, will, and inspiration."
AE saw much of this kind of sacrifice during the Rebellion and the
Civil War, but he saw little of it in the cause of peace.

VI   *America and the United States*

It was unfortunate that AE did not visit America before 1928, for
he had much to give America and it had much to give him. St. John
Ervine's judgment that AE needed to travel was correct; AE had
become insulated by his constant contact with Ireland and its
problems, and his four visits to the United States between 1928 and
1934 provided the change of intellectual climate that he needed.
But in 1928, when AE was already sixty-one years old, and had only
seven more years to live, the purpose of his first trip was to secure

funds to keep *the Irish Statesman* alive. He left Ireland in January and returned at the end of March with enough money to accomplish his purpose; *The Irish Statesman* lived two more years. In June, 1929, he returned to America to receive an honorary doctorate from Yale University.[10] His third tour in 1930 and 1931, during which he lectured at colleges and universities and before civic groups across the country, was made chiefly in order to raise money for the care of his wife, who was afflicted by her last illness.

This longest and most strenuous tour took him all over the United States, from New York City to California and from Louisiana to Canada. He visited not only such large cities as San Francisco and Chicago, but also smaller cities such as Wooster, Ohio, and Grand Rapids, Michigan. He met such famous persons as Alfred Smith, Nicholas Murray Butler, Robinson Jeffers, and Robert Millikan. He made speeches over the radio, addressed audiences at colleges and universities, met with groups of business men, and made quite an impact on his audiences wherever he went. He liked the West better than the East, but he felt that California with its gentle climate would "rot one's faculties." AE was impressed by the kindness of the people, by the country's immense distances, and by the great activity of the nation.[11] He found that many people knew his poems and his *Candle of Vision;* the committee that invited him to the United States distributed *The National Being* by the thousands; the businessmen with whom he met liked his peculiar blend of poetry and economics.[12]

AE's final visit to the United States occurred in December, 1934, at the invitation of the Franklin Delano Roosevelt administration, for the purpose of advising the Department of Agriculture about its rural policies. During AE's visit, he was introduced to President Franklin Delano roosevelt by his long-time friend, Henry A. Wallace, then Secretary of Agriculture. AE also visited his son Diarmuid in Chicago and then cut short his trip to return to England because of illness.[13] He wrote in a letter to Weekes (January 29, 1935) that he had been asked to go to New Mexico and Arizona to meet Indians there and explain to them his ideas on cooperative agriculture. The head of the Indian Department believed that AE's mystical nature would enable him to reach the Indians, whose religious ideas were similar to AE's. AE had been greatly tempted to go but could not do so because of his health.[14]

AE's impression of the United States that were published in *The Irish Statesman* were written before 1930, the date of the demise of that paper; and his views were based chiefly on his first and second journeys. His reactions to his third and fourth journeys are to be found in Eglinton's *Memoir*. Although he was impressed by the skyscrapers of New York and Chicago and by the friendliness and generosity of the people, he was concerned by the waste of natural resources but he had hopes for the future and for the development of American consciousness. He foresaw the social, moral, and political problems which face us today—the materialism, the lack of tradition and spiritual values—but felt that the diversity of the people would finally serve to bring about a true sense of world citizenship or, as he liked to call it, "planetary consciousness."

In a passage reminiscent of Whitman, he concludes his article "America and the Americans" with this hope: "I imagine centuries in which the higher minds in the States a noble sense of world duty, a world consciousness, will struggle with mass mentality and gradually pervade it, to establish there, and in the world, perhaps, the idea that all humanity are the children of one King, or at least to make so noble an idea part of the heritage of those who come after, until, finally, as it must in the ages, it becomes the dominant idea in world consciousness" (178). AE's concept of the high destiny of the United States of America seems prophetic, and we who observe the scene today can only wonder if time will prove AE right. He defined clearly the basic problem of the United States in the twentieth century, the problem summed up in the concept of "the American Dream." The question is whether or not the United States can and will provide the leadership for a world based on brotherhood, or if it will succumb to its many social and economic problems, deriving from the very source of its strength, the diversity of its peoples.

A number of miscellaneous observations summarize AE's view of America and Americans. Architecture was the chief American art. The people were kind and generous, but wasteful. Women had a high standard of good taste in dress, but AE objected to their use of lipstick. The women were charming and eager intellectually; the men were lavish in their generosity and were also strongly romantic and idealistic. But, in his review of Sinclair Lewis's *Elmer Gantry*, AE voices another view of America, possibly a superficial one, that echoes the nineteenth-century European idea that American literature was either decadent or undeveloped. He seemed to feel that the only literature in America of any value was the religious literature of the Transcendental writers and that the secular literature of America had lost touch with the past. He saw in *Elmer*

Gantry an indication that religion in America was decadent and that the arts, which sprang from religious origins in Europe, had eventually been deprived of their religious heritage in America. Referring to the myth of Apollo, in which he is driven from the world of the gods and lives with swineherds, AE makes the following judgment: "Divinity in exile in America has been herding with the Barnums" (294). In other words, religious forms in America had the aspect of the circus and had become a mode of entertainment;

The secular literature of the States has almost lost affinities with the past. Its moods are without spiritual ancestry, and as the secular culture became more secular the mood of the people reeled further and further away from the spiritual, and at last the aristocratic language of religion became so remote from the mentality of the average man that, if he was to be interested at all, religion had to talk in a kind of slang, do its turn in the pulpit just as the acrobat does his turn on the stage. The re-conquest of America for the spirit is an adventure that the most heroic might contemplate with misgiving. The only way of recalling the soul to beauty is by the creation of beauty. (295)

In AE's most perceptive article in *The Irish Statesman* about American culture, he sees the United States as being mainly materialistic, unable to derive the true historical and spiritual significance of Europe, separated from the past, but possessed with tremendous possibilities for the future. The Transcendentalists—Emerson, Thoreau, Whitman, Melville, and Hawthorne—are the only American writers who have developed "planetary consciousness."

Because other writers who came after these authors have been Naturalistic and materialistic, AE suggests that America needs a prophet like Plato, Dante, or Shakespeare to bring the United States to the fulfillment of its promise (319 - 23). As for its promise, AE seemingly believed that the only hope for the world lay in America because Europe was exhausted, but America was new and vital. If the United States did not become too deeply immersed in materialism, this nation could lead the way to the "world consciousness" that AE's mystical belief held to be the only possible creative world view. To AE, the United States was not an extension of European culture but a new departure; and he felt that from its power and its diversity would come "the next world truth, planetary consciousness, universal brotherhood of man. . . ."[15]

CHAPTER 8

Conclusion

THE extensive contributions of George William Russell to Ireland and to the world outside of Ireland may be divided into those that pertained to his life and times, and those that are of lasting value. As we have shown, he was a versatile, dynamic personality, capable in many areas of human activity. In the realms of art, journalism, economics, and politics his influence was great and endures to the present day. He is still well known in Britain and Ireland, and it is not uncommon to find there persons who have a knowledge of him and his work, or even persons who knew him or his associates. His relative obscurity in the United States today must not be permitted to serve as an indicator of his importance or lack of it.

In the history of Irish arts and letters, AE has a lasting place. He was one of the leaders of the Irish literary Renaissance, and one of the founders of the Irish dramatic movement and the famed Abbey Theatre, which is still reckoned one of the outstanding centers of dramatic art in the world. Not only did he practice the arts himself, but he also encouraged some of the great writers of Ireland who have come to prominence since his death—Padraic Colum, James Stephens, C. P. Curran, Frank O'Connor, Sean O'Faolain, and Liam O'Flaherty, to name a few. He was a friend and colleague of W. B. Yeats, and Yeats had great respect for AE, though they did not always agree in their artistic opinions.

In the economic and political life of his country AE was also a powerful figure, as we have shown in those chapters dealing with his work for the cooperative movement and his efforts for Home Rule. There is no doubt that his work as an agricultural organizer and as assistant secretary of the Irish Agricultural Organization Society left an indelible mark on Ireland. Later, with the coming of the Dublin Strike, his interests and efforts extended to the problems of labor, and he was ultimately drawn into the struggle over Ireland's freedom from Britain. His efforts on behalf of Irish independence in the Home Rule Convention of 1917, and his writings which followed, concerning conscription of Irishmen, the Treaty, the partition, and the Civil War, all proved him to be the conscience of his country. He was that greatly needed but inadequately respected figure in every nation, the philosophical statesman. There is evidence that he was trusted by the most extreme groups in that conflict, and the fact that he was invited by Lloyd George, the Prime Minister of England to consult with him in London concerning the problem of Irish independence, indicates that his opinions were respected. It is possible that his negotiations with Lord Northcliffe, publisher of the *Daily Mail*, may have contributed to bringing American opinion to bear on Britain, so as to bring about a settlement of the Anglo-Irish War. But it is certain that his candid writings of the period in English journals brought the British public to an awareness of the need for Irish independence, and to a recognition of the Irish nation as a distinct entity.

In the field of journalism, he was the editor of two important Irish journals, *The Irish Homestead* and *The Irish Statesman* from 1905 to 1930. The files of these papers constitute an historical record of the times, one which can be relied on because of AE's known objectivity. Also, as an editor he was in a position to encourage young writers by publishing their works, and he did so with unfailing enthusiasm. As we have shown in the last chapter, his writings for *The Irish Statesman* reveal his ability not only as an editor, but also as a writer. Journalistic writing is usually casual, transient, and impermanent, but AE's journalistic efforts were unusual in producing writing that was philosophical and literary. One can read his articles today with as much interest and pleasure as when they were written.

We may also say that AE's contributions were of lasting importance. His writings represent an objective and unprejudiced record of the times and for the historian are of great value. His poetry, though not of the highest quality compared with the touchstones of English and Irish poetry, is excellent, and as religious poetry it has lasting value. His efforts in poetry and painting are a source of inspiration for artists everywhere, chiefly for their integrity and honesty. His masterpiece of economic and political writing, *The National Being*, is still a guide for all who are interested in develop-

ing a sane national government. And his visionary writings will
always represent the highest kind of human experience, the keen
perception of the divine in all its splendor.

But above all, AE remains for us the philosopher, and it is not at
all unusual that he should regard Socrates as the epitome of human
wisdom. One of his last and finest poems might well serve as our
final view of him, at least for the present:

> Although the merchant be your care
> The mart or field, do not forget—
> To leave a glory on the air
> When the red Gaelic sun has set—
>
> Some prophet must have cried a word
> The hurrying world will pause to hear.
> Even for the unfaltering sword
> No one will hold your memory dear.
>
> The Greece of Pericles is cold:
> Yet still there shines beyond its seas
> The wisdom Diotima told
> In the rapt ear of Socrates.[1]

Notes and References

Chapter One

1. C. C. Coates, *Some Less Known Chapters in the Life of AE (George Russell)*. Lecture delivered in Belfast, 1936. Privately printed, (Dublin, 1939), p. 10.
2. John Eglinton, *A Memoir of AE* (London, 1937), pp. 102 - 03.
3. St. John G. Ervine, *Some Impressions of My Elders* (New York, 1922), p. 27.
4. Diarmuid Russell, "AE," *Atlantic Monthly*, CLXXI (February, 1943), 52.
5. *Ibid.*, p. 55.
6. Ervine, p. 25.
7. Eglinton, *Memoir*, p. 101.
8. *Ibid.*, pp. 154 - 55.
9. Diarmuid Russell, p. 52.
10. Monk Gibbon, *The Living Torch* (New York, 1938), p. 12.
11. Henry Summerfield, *That Myriad-Minded Man: A Biography of G. W. Russell—"AE"* (Totowa, N. J., 1975), p. 154.
12. Eglinton, *Memoir*, pp. 182 - 83.
13. Diarmuid Russell, p. 55.
14. Gibbon, pp. 15 - 16. Translation from the French by Robert B. Davis. Quoted from Simone Téry's *L'Isle de Bardes*.
15. Eglinton, *Memoir*, p. 84.
16. Diarmuid Russell, p. 56.
17. *Ibid.*, p. 54.
18. Gibbon, p. 40. From *The Enneads of Plotinus*, translated by Stephen MacKenna, second edition; revised by B. S. Page (London, 1956), the First Ennead, Sixth Tractate, Section 9.
19. Oliver St. John Gogarty, "An Angelic Anarchist," *Colby College Quarterly*, IV, 2 (May, 1955), pp. 26 - 27.
20. Diarmuid Russell, p. 57.
21. Summerfield, p. 3. See also Eglinton, *Memoir*, p. 21.
22. Summerfield, p. 19.
23. *Ibid.*, p. 6.
24. *Ibid.*, pp. 11 - 12.
25. *Ibid.*, pp. 16, 93.
26. *Ibid.*, p. 22.
27. *Ibid.*, pp. 23 - 24.

28. Eglinton, *Memoir*, p. 52.

29. The *Tuatha de Danaan* means "the people of the Goddess Dana." Dana is the Irish mother of the gods; thus the *Tuatha de Danaan* are the earliest people of Ireland. They are also called the *Sidhe* (pronounced something like *shee*), or "the people of the wind." See George William Russell, *Collected Poems* (London, 1935), p. 428, and T. E. G. Powell, *The Celts* (London, 1963), pp. 126 - 28.

30. Summerfield, p. 74.

31. *Ibid.*, p. 59.

32. *The Candle of Vision*, pp. 73 - 75.

33. Eglinton, *Memoir*, pp. 9, 27. See also Summerfield, pp. 14, 31. Summerfield says that AE's two names represented the two parts of his being; "George William Russell" was his "superficial, personal self, a transient creation of this life," while "AE" represented "the Logos incarnated in human form." See also James H. Cousins, "AE: Poet of the Spirit," *Theosophist*, LVI (September, 1935), p. 596.

34. "Draper" is an English term for a dealer in cloth, "dry goods" in American English.

35. Coates, p. 5; Summerfield, p. 9.

36. Summerfield, pp. 33, 60.

37. Diarmuid Russell, p. 52. See also Summerfield, pp. 89 - 94, 99 - 103, and Ms. letters to Charles Weekes from AE in the Armagh County Museum.

38. Summerfield, pp. 82, 95.

39. *Ibid.*, pp. 125 - 26.

40. *Ibid.*, pp. 119 - 22.

41. Lucy Kingsley Porter, "Introduction," *AE's Letters to Mínanlábáin* (New York, 1937), pp. 1 - 3. See also Eglinton, *Memoir*, p. 113.

42. Summerfield, p. 114.

43. *Ibid.*, p. 104. Quoted from *The Splendid Years* (Dublin, 1955), p. 29. See also Gibbon, p. 22.

44. Diarmuid Russell, p. 53. See also Gibbon, p. 65.

45. Summerfield, pp. 160 - 62.

46. *Ibid.*, p. 162.

47. "The Crime and the Punishment," *Irish Worker* (November 1, 1913), p. 3. Summerfield, p. 163.

48. Summerfield, p. 174.

49. *Ibid.*, pp. 156 - 57.

50. *Ibid.*, p. 166.

51. *Ibid.*, p. 178.

52. *Ibid.*, pp. 181 - 88. *Sinn Fein* (pronounced *shin fayn*) in Irish means "we ourselves" and was the name of the Nationalist political party founded by Arthur Griffith in 1907. Irish Nationalism assumes that Ireland is a separate nation, never willingly included in the British Empire. Its original inhabitants were Gaels, and the language they spoke is the origin of

modern Erse, Irish, or Gaelic, as it is variously called. The Unionists, obviously, were in favor of union with Great Britain.

53.   *Ibid.*, p. 189.
54.   *Ibid.*, p. 195.
55.   *Ibid.*, p. 196.
56.   Alan Denson (ed.), *Letters from AE* (London, 1961), pp. 158 - 63.
57.   Ervine, p. 57.
58.   Eglinton, *Memoir*, pp. 283 - 85.
59.   Gibbon, pp. 20 - 21. Quoted from F. R. Higgins.

Chapter Two

1.   M. J. Bonn, "Reminiscences of AE," in Alan Denson (ed.), *Printed Writings by George W. Russell (AE): A Bibliography* (Evanston, Ill., 1961), p. 19.
2.   *The Irish Theosophist*, III, 6 (March 15, 1895), 101. Reprinted in *Three Mystic Poets: A Study of W. B. Yeats, AE, and Rabindranath Tagore*, by Abinash Chandra Bose (Kolhapur, 1945), p. 73. This book contains an excellent explanation of mysticism.
3.   *The Hero in Man* (London, 1910, second edition), p. 17.
4.   *Renewal of Youth* (London, 1911), VII, 18. Page numbers for future references are given in parentheses in the text.
5.   *The Candle of Vision*, pp. 4 - 5. Page numbers for future references are given in parentheses.
6.   "The pilgrim of eternity" is Shelley's name for Byron in *Adonais*.
7.   W. B. Yeats, *Autobiographies* (New York, 1927), pp. 324 - 25.
8.   Helen of Troy derives from Classical myth; Deirdre and the Red Branch both derive from Irish myth.
9.   *Song and Its Fountains* (New York, 1932). Page numbers for future references are given in parentheses.
10.   *Collected Poems* (London, 1935), p. 72.
11.   See Denson's *Bibliography*, p. 95, for a list of the poems explicated in *Song and Its Fountains* and the pages where they appear in *Collected Poems*. Page numbers refer to the 1931 edition.

Chapter Three

1.   Eglinton, *Memoir*, pp. 178 - 79. See also Eglinton, "The Story of AE," *Irish Literary Portraits* (London, 1935), pp. 50 - 51.
2.   James and Margaret Cousins, *We Two Together* (Madras, 1950), p. 33.
3.   Ernest A. Boyd, *Appreciations and Depreciations* (Dublin and London, 1917), pp. 28 - 29. Chapter II of this book is entitled "AE: Mystic and Economist."
4.   Gibbon, p. 53.
5.   James Stephens's obituary of AE in *The Observer*, July 21, 1935.

6.   Clifford Bax, *Some I Knew Well* (London, 1951), pp. 85 - 86. Chapter 9 is entitled "AE: The Strayed Angel," pp. 77 - 96. Contains a photograph of the marble bust by Oliver Sheppard.

7.   Sean O'Casey, *Inishfallen Fare Thee Well* (New York, 1949), p. 269.

8.   Ernest A. Boyd, *Ireland's Literary Renaissance* (New York, 1916), p. 225. Chapter 10 is entitled "The Dublin Mystics."

9.   Bose, p. 87.

10.   Letter to Weekes from AE, dated December 1, 1926. (Armagh County Museum Collection.)

11.   Letter to Weekes from AE, December 14, 1926, (Armagh County Museum Collection.)

12.   Eglinton, *Memoir*, pp. 14, 32, 176. See also Grace Jameson, "Irish Poets of Today and Blake," *Publications of the Modern Language Association*, LIII (June, 1938), 575.

13.   Eglinton, *Memoir*, pp. 103 - 04.

14.   Diarmuid Russell, p. 56.

15.   Bose, p. 30.

16.   *Collected Poems*, p. vii. Page numbers for future references are given in parentheses.

17.   "The House of the Titans," title poem in *The House of the Titans and Other Poems* (New York, 1934), pp. 3 - 35.

18.   See Notes in *Collected Poems*, pp. 428 - 30.

19.   The Titans were the first beings on earth. In Classical mythology, they were the six sons and six daughters of Heaven and Earth.

20.   *House of the Titans*, pp. 57 - 58.

21.   The Wild Geese were "men of great families who served under foreign standards after 1691 because of the penal laws against Catholics." *Notes to Selected Poems and Two Plays of William Butler Yeats*, ed., M. L. Rosenthal (New York, 1962), p. 213. Yeats mentions the "wild geese" in "September 1913": "Was it for this the wild geese spread/The grey wing upon every tide . . . ?"

22.   *House of the Titans*, pp. 46 - 55. Numbers in parentheses refer to pages in this book. Mr. Denson reports that Professor Bergin informed him that this poem was the result of AE's reading of Walter Raleigh's book on Shakespeare.

23.   *Collected Poems*, p. 133.

Chapter Four

1.   *Deirdre*, No. 4 of the Tower Press Booklets, Second Series (Dublin, 1907).

2.   Myles Dillon, *Early Irish Literature* (Chicago, 1948), pp. 13 - 16. See also George Brandon Saul, *The Shadow of the Three Queens* (Harrisburg, Pa., 1953), pp. 74 - 77.

3.   *The Mask of Apollo* (Dublin and London, 1905), pp. 3 - 6. See *Bibliography*, p. 60, for a list of the stories and record of publication. Page

numbers for future references are given in parentheses.

    4. Concerning Lilith, see the following: (1) "Lilith," *Oxford Companion to English Literature;* (2) *An Encyclopaedia of Occultism,* ed. Lewis Spence (New York, 1960) p. 251; (3) *The Holy Kabbahlah,* A. E. Waite (New Hyde Park, N.Y., n.d.), pp. 258, 288, 289, 419; (4) Isaiah 34: 14, where Lilith is translated in various editions "screeth-owl," "night-hag," or "night-monster." She was one of the four mothers of demons and is generally considered a temptress.

    5. AE's letter to Charles Weekes, December 1, 1926. (Armagh County Museum Collection.)

    6. *The Interpreters* (London, 1922), p. viii. Page numbers for future references are given in parentheses.

    7. Henry Summerfield has defined these relationships as follows: Lavelle is AE, Rian represents the young Yeats or possibly John Hughes, Culain is Larkin, Leroy is very much like Gogarty and James Stephens, Heyt is similar to William Murphy, and Brehon is Standish O'Grady. See Henry Summerfield, *That Myriad-Minded Man—A.E.* (Totowa, N.J., 1976), pp. 212 - 13. See also Richard M. Kain and James H. O'Brien, *George Russell (A.E.)* (Lewisburgh, Pa., 1976), pp. 45 - 46, where it is noted that Leroy is suggestive of George Moore.

    8. *Collected Poems,* p. 368. Published originally as a pamphlet in December, 1919 (Denson 37). Cf. Emerson's "Brahma":

> If the red slayer think he slays,
>   Or if the slain think he is slain,
> They know not well the subtle ways
>   I keep, and pass, and turn again.

    9. Eglinton, *Memoir,* p. 240.

    10. *The Avatars* (New York, 1933), p. vii. Numbers in parentheses refer to this volume.

Chapter Five

    1. AE's letter to Charles Weekes, December 1, 1926. (Armagh County Museum Collection.)

    2. *The Irish Theosophist,* V (January 15 and February 15, 1897), 66 - 69 and 85 - 89. Privately printed in March, 1897, by AE. Page numbers for future references are given in parentheses.

    3. *Ibid.,* (April 15 and May 15, 1897), 127 - 31 and 148 - 52. Privately printed in May, 1897, by AE. Numbers in parentheses refer to this volume.

    4. An address delivered at the Annual General Meeting of the Irish Agricultural Organization Society on December 10, 1909 (Dublin, 1910). Numbers in parentheses refer to this volume.

    5. *Co-operation and Nationality* (Dublin, 1912). Numbers in parentheses refer to this volume.

6. *The National Being* (Dublin and London, 1916). Numbers in parentheses refer to this volume.

7. See Summerfield, p. 194, where he says that Professor Eoil McNeil showed that this theory was false.

8. The term *Ulster* refers to one of the four provinces of Ireland in ancient times. Ulster was the northern province. The others were Leinster (east), Munster (south), and Connaught (west). In modern times, Ulster has become synonymous with the North of Ireland, or the six northern counties in Northern Ireland. The Ulster Volunteers were for the Union; the Irish Volunteers, for Home Rule.

9. "An Angelic Anarchist," *Colby Library Quarterly*, IV, 2 (May, 1955), 24 - 26.

Chapter Six

1. See Denson, *Bibliography*, pp. 70 - 72 (Denson 24).

2. "To the Masters of Dublin: An Open Letter," reprinted from the *Irish Times*, Tuesday, October 13, 1913. (Denson 22) See also *Letters from AE*. p. 85.

3. "The Tragedy of Labour in Dublin," *Letters from AE*, p. 93.

4. *Ibid.*, p. 94.

5. T. A. Jackson, *Ireland Her Own* (New York, 1947), pp. 364 - 66.

6. *Ibid.*, p. 377. See also Edgar Holt, *Protest in Arms* (New York, 1960), pp. 51 - 52.

7. Denson, *Letters from AE*, p. 99.

8. *Ibid.*, pp. 117 - 18.

9. Holt, pp. 82 - 83; Jackson, pp. 378 - 79.

10. Gibbon, *The Living Torch*, p. 167.

11. *Letters from AE*, p. 97.

12. *Salutation, A Poem on the Irish Rebellion of 1916* (London, January, 1917). (Denson 32)

13. Later published in *The Irish Home-Rule Convention* (New York, 1917), pp. 97 - 155. Page numbers in parentheses refer to this volume. See *Bibliography*, pp. 81 and 112, for a description of this volume.

14. See Chapter One, note 52.

15. Irish nationalism assumes that the original inhabitants were the Gaels, a branch of the Celtic group. Hence the terms Irish, Gaelic, and Celtic are often used interchangeably to describe the Irish People. The Welsh are Celtic, but not Gaelic; Irish, Scots Gaelic, and Manx all belong to the Goidelic group of languages; Welsh, Breton, and Cornish belong to the Brittanic group. See the introduction to *Teach Yourself Irish* by Myles Dillon and Donncha O Cróinín (London, 1961), p. ix.

Though the Anglo-Saxons never invaded Ireland, in the twelfth century the country was invaded and settled by the Normans, and the Scots and English settled in Ulster in the late sixteenth and early seventeenth centuries. This accounts for the mixture of Gaelic, Norman, Scots, and English in the present population of Ireland.

16.   It is interesting to note that Irish patriots have not always been pure Irish: Wolfe Tone was Anglo-Irish; Pearse's father was English; Constance Markiewicz was from the Anglo-Irish Ascendency.

17.   See Denson, *Letters from AE*, p. 241, for a short biography. Balfour was Chief Secretary for Ireland (1887 - 91), Prime Minister of England (1902 - 05), First Lord of the Admiralty (1915), and Foreign Secretary (1916 - 19).

18.   *Letters from AE*, pp. 112 - 114.

19.   Holt, *Protest in Arms*, p. 151.

20.   Letter to Edward MacLysaght, December, 1917, *Letters from AE*, p. 134.

21.   Letter from Sir Horace Plunkett to AE, February 2, 1918, *Letters from AE*, pp. 136 - 37. AE's reply, p. 137.

22.   *Ibid.*, pp. 137 - 38.

23   Holt, pp. 151 - 61.

24.   Eglinton, *Memoir*, p. 126.

25.   *Ibid.*, p. 135.

26.   *Letters from AE*, pp. 141 - 44.

27.   Holt, p. 151. Collins and De Valera, leaders of Sinn Fein, later split over the subject of the Treaty. Collins became a leader of the pro-Treaty party and De Valera a leader of the anti-Treaty party. Collins was killed in an ambush during the Civil War. De Valera, who lived to become one of the great leaders of the Irish Free State, eventually became Prime Minister of Ireland. See *Letters from AE*, pp. 248 - 49, for a brief biography of De Valera. For Michael Collins, see Rex Taylor's book, *Michael Collins* (London, 1961).

28.   Published by *The Irish Homestead* in December, 1920 (Denson 38).

29.   *The Economics of Ireland, and the Policy of the British Government* (New York, 1921), p. 11. Reprinted from *The Freeman* (New York, April 28, 1920). See also AE's letter to *The Times* (London, March 25, 1921), "Irish Finance, Effects of the Act," *Letters from AE*, pp. 152 - 54.

30.   *Letters from AE*, p. 154.

31.   *Economics of Ireland*, p. 20. This is the general opinion of many writers at the time of the partition. Two authors who wrote on this subject were Eoin MacNeill, "The Ulster Difficulty," and Henry Harrison, "The Irish Case Considered," both filed in the National Library of Ireland under I 94109 P 3. Harrison's article (London, 1920) was endorsed by Sir Horace Plunkett.

32.   *The Inner and the Outer Ireland* (Dublin, 1921), pp. 4 - 5, reprinted from *Pearson's Magazine* (New York, May, 1921), 399 - 402.

33.   Holt, p. 258.

34.   *Ireland and The Empire at Court of Conscience* (Dublin, 1921).

35.   First printed in *The Sociological Review* (London, April, 1922). Later reprinted as a pamphlet.

36.   The trouble seems to have arisen chiefly in the cities (Londonderry, Belfast, and Armagh) as a result of alleged religious discrimination and

religious differences, but the historical antecedents still exist in differences
of nationality, religion, and origin. The other four counties are Armagh,
Down, Londonderry, and Antrim.

37.   *Ireland, Past and Future*, p. 17.

38.   *Letters from AE*, pp. 158 - 62.

39.   *Ibid.*, p. 162.

40.   Eglinton, *Memoir*, p. 148.

41.   "Twenty-five years of Irish Nationality," *Foreign Affairs*, VII
(January 1929), 204 - 20.

42.   *Ibid.*, 211.

Chapter Seven

1.   Eglinton, *Memoir*, pp. 149 - 51.

2.   *Ibid.*, p. 72.

3.   *Ibid.*, pp. 190 - 91.

4.   *Ibid.*, p. 151.

5.   *Letters from AE*, p. 167.

6.   *The Living Torch*, pp. 66 - 67.

7.   References to *The Living Torch* are given in the text in parentheses.
See Denson's *Bibliography*, pp. 101 - 04 for the sources of these articles.

8.   *Letters from AE*, p. 209.

9.   For Jung's definition of the collective unconscious, see C. G. Jung,
The Archetypes and the Collective Unconscious, translated by R. F. C.
Hull. Bollingen Series 20. Pantheon Books. Volume IX of *Collected Works*
(New York, 1959).

10.   Eglinton, *Memoir*, pp. 192, 196.

11.   *Ibid.*, pp. 214 - 16.

12.   *Ibid.*, p. 218.

13.   *Ibid.*, pp. 273 - 80.

14.   *Ibid.*, p. 279.

15.   Robert Collis, *The Silver Fleece: An Autobiography* (London, 1936),
p. 265.

Chapter Eight

1.   *Collected Poems*, p. 351. Diotima was the priestess of Mantinea to
whom Socrates refers in *The Symposium* as his teacher. In the poem she
symbolizes wisdom as opposed to commerce, war, and worldly affairs.

Selected Bibliography

PRIMARY SOURCES

The Avatars. New York: Macmillan and Company, 1933.
The Candle of Vision. London: Macmillan and Company, 1919.
Collected Poems. London: Macmillan and Company, 1935.
Co-operation and Nationality. Dublin: Maunsel and Company, 1912.
Deirdre. Dublin: Maunsel and Company, 1907.
The House of the Titans and Other Poems. New York: The Macmillan Company, 1934.
The Interpreters. London: Macmillan and Company, 1922.
The Mask of Apollo. Dublin: Whaley and Company; London: Macmillan and Company, 1905.
The National Being. Dublin and London: Maunsel and Company, 1916.
Song and Its Fountains. New York: The Macmillan Company, 1932.

The Collected Works. Colin Smythe Limited, Publishers, Gerrards Cross, Buckinghamshire, England, has announced that it will publish the Collected Edition of the Works of AE, with the first volumes scheduled to appear in 1977.

SELECTED BACKGROUND MATERIALS

CONNERY, DONALD S. *The Irish*. New York: Simon and Schuster, 1970. A good brief description of the Irish people and Irish life. Covers recent developments in Northern Ireland up to the explosive developments of 1969, which revived the traditional hostilities between Catholic and Protestant, Nationalist and Unionist.

CURTIS, EDMUND. *A History of Ireland*. London: Methuen and Company; New York: Barnes and Noble, 1964. University Paperbacks, No. 23. A good single-volume history of Ireland from the origins up to the Treaty of 1922.

CORKERY, DANIEL. *The Fortunes of the Irish Language*. Cork: The Mercier Press, 1968. A history of the Irish language from prehistoric times to 1919.

DILLON, MYLES. *Early Irish Literature*. Chicago: University of Chicago Press, 1948. A thorough and authoritative treatment of the legendary and mythological literature of Ireland. No bibliography, but the preface contains other titles on the subject.

DILLON, MYLES and Ó CROÍNÍN, DONNCHA. *Teach Yourself Irish*. London:

155

English Universities Press, 1962. The introduction gives a brief
description of the Celtic family of languages, including Irish and its
dialects.

HOLT, EDGAR. *Protest in Arms*. New York: Coward-McCann, 1960. A
precise description of the events of the period from 1916 to 1923, and
the Irish revolt against England and the Civil War. Well illustrated.

JACKSON, T. A. *Ireland Her Own*. New York: International Publishers,
1960. The story of how Ireland became a part of the British Empire
and of the efforts to dissolve that association. Concludes with the
Constitution of 1937, which created the independent and sovereign
state of Eire.

Ó CUÍV, BRIAN. *A View of the Irish Language*. Dublin: Stationery Office,
1969. A collection of articles by various persons, concerning various
aspects of the Irish language. See especially, "The Irish Language
and the Languages of the World," by Kenneth H. Jackson, pp. 1 - 10.

POWELL, T. G. E. *The Celts*. London: Thames and Hudson, 1963. One of
a series entitled, *Ancient Peoples and Places*, which describes the
Celtic peoples. Well illustrated, with a list of museums containing
Celtic materials.

SAUL, GEORGE BRANDON. *The Shadow of the Three Queens*. Harrisburg,
Pa.: The Stackpole Company, 1953. A handbook for the study of Early Irish literature, also containing a note on the Irish Language.

SECONDARY SOURCES

BOSE, ABINASH CHANDRA. *Three Mystic Poets: A Study of W. B. Yeats, AE,
and Rabindranath Tagore*. Kolhapur: School and College Bookstall,
1945. Excellent for its definition of mysticism and background study
of the mystical ideas of AE, Yeats, and Tagore.

BOYD, ERNEST A. *Ireland's Literary Renaissance*. New York: John Lane
Co., 1916. See Chapter 10, "The Dublin Mystics," for a good
background study of the literary movement and AE's part in it. AE
commended the author for his accuracy.

————. *Appreciations and Depreciations*. Dublin: The Talbot Press, Ltd.;
London: T. Fisher Unwin, Ltd., 1917. Chapter II is devoted to AE,
and is entitled, " 'AE': Mystic and Economist." A good early study of
AE's fusion of economics and mysticism. AE said of this book, that
"Boyd is conscientious and accurate in his facts."

COATES, C. C. *Some Less Known Chapters in the Life of A. E. (George
Russell)*. Dublin: Privately Printed, 1939. The author is AE's
childhood friend, Caroline Rea, from whom we learn much about
AE's childhood and youth.

COLLIS, ROBERT. *The Silver Fleece: An Autobiography*. London: Thomas
Nelson and Sons, Ltd., 1936. Chapter 16, "AE," is a description of AE
in his later years. Collis was a companion on an ocean voyage from
America to Europe.

DENSON, ALAN. *Printed Writings by George W. Russell (AE): A Bibliography*. Evanston: Northwestern University Press, 1961. Any study of AE should begin with this work. Besides proving a list of all of AE's works, it contains much additional useful information, including a note on AE's painting by Thomas Bodkin, and lists of AE's paintings.

DENSON, ALAN (ED.). *Letters from AE*. London, New York, and Toronto: Abelard-Schumann, 1961. Contains in addition to the most complete collection of AE's letters available, a foreword by Dr. Monk Gibbon, chronological tables, notes on the letters, biographical sketches of many of AE's contemporaries, and "Notes on Lurgan, Armagh, and District in the Late Nineteenth Century," by T. G. F. Paterson. It is typical of Mr. Denson's meticulous scholarship.

EGLINTON, JOHN. *A Memoir of AE*. London: Macmillan and Company, 1937. The first full-length biography of AE. Alan Denson says that "despite factual errors the Memoir remains the sole indispensable source for students of AE's life." Summerfield's biography has now surpassed it, but it is still valuable for its immediacy.

ERVINE, ST. JOHN G. *Some Impressions of My Elders*. New York: The Macmillan Company, 1922. "AE (George William Russell)" contains a very critical description of AE and perhaps completes the record. The author is particularly critical of AE's theory of national divinity as presented in *The National Being*.

FIGGIS, DARRELL. *AE (George William Russell): A Study of a Man and a Nation*. Dublin and London: Maunsel and Company, 1916. In spite of the fact that AE disapproved of this book, it remains the first book-length biography of AE. See Denson's description of the book in his *Bibliography*, p. 188, and his note on Figgis in *Letters from AE*, p. 250.

GIBBON, MONK (ED.). *The Living Torch*. New York: The Macmillan Company, 1938. An edited collection of the writings of AE for *The Irish Statesman*. The introduction, entitled "AE," is a valuable contribution by a friend of AE to the record of his life and work. Contains descriptions of portraits and busts of AE and also of his paintings.

KAIN, RICHARD M. and O'BRIEN, JAMES H. *George Russell (A. E.)*. Lewisburg: Bucknell University Press, 1976. The first three chapters by Professor Kain provide a good short biographical sketch, and the last two chapters by Professor O'Brien are an interesting treatment of AE's poetry and his theosophical beliefs.

O'CASEY, SEAN. *Inishfallen Fare Thee Well*. New York: The Macmillan Company, 1949. See Chapter 15, "Dublin's Glittering Guy," for a devastating portrait of AE as a humbug who pretended to humility. Though this must be read with care, it represents the other side of the picture that we usually get of AE.

PORTER, LUCY KINGSLEY (ED.). *AE's Letters to Mínanlábáin*. New York:

The Macmillan Company, 1937. Collection of AE's letters that supplements Denson's *Letters from AE*. The introduction contains valuable information about AE's last years.

RUSSELL, DIARMUID. "AE," *Atlantic Monthly*, CLXXI (February, 1943), 51 - 57. Detailed view of AE as a father and family man, by his son. Particularly good for its treatment of AE's mind and personality.

SUMMERFIELD, HENRY. *That Myriad-Minded Man: A Biography of G. W. Russell—"A.E."* Totowa, N.J.: Rowman and Littlefield, 1975. The most complete biography of AE available, with extensive detail and meticulous research. Contains many excellent photographs.

YEATS, WILLIAM BUTLER. *Autobiographies*. New York: The Macmillan Company, 1927. Gives valuable insights into early life of AE and the relations between Yeats and AE.

Index